Living of
Natural Causes

Essays by

KADZI MUTIZWA

AUTHOR'S NOTE

I've been keeping a personal journal (a Microsoft Word document that is now more than 1,800 single-spaced pages) since the early 2000s and, I gotta say, it really came in handy for an undertaking like this. That said, much of the material in this essay collection has been reconstructed from memory. And many of my impressions aren't necessarily literal.

There's more.

Some of the names and identifying details in this book have been changed. A measure, in addition to the general vagueness you'll notice in a number of sections, that's meant to help protect people's privacy as much as possible, without overly sacrificing the bigger-picture storytelling and thematic development. I wish I could tell you more in many of the pages that follow, but I can't/won't.

TABLE OF CONTENTS

For my father, Tasiyana Mutizwa

And you'll say girl [did] you kick some butt
And I'll say I don't really remember
But my fingers are sore
And my voice is too.

—Ani DiFranco

THE STATE VS. KADZI MUTIZWA

Whenever I walk up a certain strip of Columbus Avenue, I still see the goofy grin of the truck driver who pulled over and invited me to hop in and smoke up with him one morning. His offer was timely, my nerves were shot, his smile intrigued me, and I had little to lose. I shook my head no and kept moving.

By morning, I mean sometime around 5:30 a.m. on a Sunday, the Sun just beginning to make its big debut. There's now (as of 2021) a bank, a bakery, a Chipotle, a chain burger joint, and a Home Goods on that side of the street, but at the time this area was nothing more than a construction site alongside a narrow pedestrian pathway. Columbus Avenue is my favorite busy street on Manhattan's Upper West Side. Broadway feels too mainstream, Amsterdam doesn't feel mainstream enough, and don't get me started about Central Park West. I'll try to go down (or, rather, up) that road in a minute.

That morning, I wasn't coming home from a party or a bar or a raunchy hook-up or any other place where a single twentysomething in the city should have spent her

Saturday night. I was on my way back from doing a favor for Maddie, a former friend, who lived in Brooklyn and too often treated me like her court jester or some other type of minion. She didn't live in the trendy part of Brooklyn that's close to the city and to the hearts of many twentysomethings who often think, and then say, things like "feels too mainstream." Maddie's part of Brooklyn involved an 85-minute (one-way) subway commute (three trains) from my Upper Manhattan apartment. When she left for a graduation party that night before this dawn, she said she wouldn't stay long. I didn't see her again for hours. I can't exactly say this was the first time something beyond low-key or run-of-the-mill came to pass during late-night/early-morning trips home from her place.

Take, for example, what went on less than six months earlier. On the Saturday night of Martin Luther King Jr. Day weekend, I trekked over the bridge to babysit her kids so she could hit the club with people I suspect were nothing like me. I have a weakness for children and travel, so up until the toilet clogged at the end of the night, the kids and I had a lovely evening. I identified with all three, but 10-year-old Lindsay was my little darling. I saw my girlhood self in her, although she seemed better adjusted to the swing of things. I wouldn't describe her as tough, just tougher than I used to be.

Once again, Maddie got home later than what our, or my, understanding had been. I was mad about the tardiness and what it represented, and knew that if I were a parent she wouldn't have volunteered to babysit for me on a nonemergency basis. I thought about accepting her halfhearted last-minute offer to sleep over. But without my pajamas, toothbrush, and Afro pick, not to mention the unreliable toilet in the apartment's only bathroom?

***

I took the subway back into the city ("At This Hour of the Night," were the only words of the conductor's service-related announcement I was able to make out) and ended up getting off the D train at Rockefeller Center, two stops too early, as if I were an out-of-towner, unfamiliar with public transportation. I *was* a little unfamiliar with public transportation because, back then, I hardly ever used it, walking pretty much everywhere I needed to go. I got to and from work, and to and from play, on foot, walking from Morningside Heights to Midtown East, the Upper West Side to the Upper East Side, South Harlem to the East Village. A compulsion I wish had more permanence, as it helped tidy up some of what happened in my head and allowed me to fit into pants and skirts that now look like doll's clothing to me.

Staying put on the platform, I waited for the next train to carry me to Columbus Circle. After almost an hour, my ride hadn't pulled into the station. I looked around and did a head count—we had a well-behaved guy of a hard-to-gauge age (one of those who could pass for both 24 and 42), yours truly, and too many agile rats to accurately tally. It might have been the coldest night of the winter thus far, the *middle of* the coldest night, and I hadn't been this spent in days.

Next thing I knew, I stormed up filthy staircases (not unlike the way Gargamel stormed around when he had a bone to pick with a Smurf), out of the station and onto still-brightly-lit Sixth Avenue, a festive fountain on my left, Radio City Music Hall up ahead. Many sections of Manhattan can come off as pristine as a beach in Bermuda, yet as electrifying as a live performance from Prince, in the hours leading up to daybreak. This was one of them.

The Columbus Circle station was a 10-minute walk away. Go straight on Sixth, turn left on Central Park South. But the way this night was going, who knew how long of a wait and how many rodents there'd be in this next underground station? I was marginally employed at that time and pathologically cheap with myself at almost all times, so the idea of springing for a cab didn't pop into my head. A $15 fare would have left me with hardly any grocery money for the coming week. As cold and tired as I was, I had nothing to wake up early for the next day or the day after that. Optimal safety, comfort, and efficiency hadn't fallen into the Unnecessary Extravagances bucket, they'd been pushed.

I can take it from here, insisted my head-voice, a loud-mouth siren that rarely pipes down. *I'm gonna walk myself all the way home*, a several-mile, round-trip hike I often did five days a week. Only not during the electrifyingly pristine hours before daybreak.

To get onto Central Park West, and into my bed, more quickly, I decided to cut through a small swath of Central Park itself. I know the west side of that park like the back of my hand and had no reservations about navigating the shortcut. The way I walked and was about to start running, it shouldn't have taken longer than five minutes. In early 2008, New York wasn't like the New York of the '70s or '80s. It was no mugger's paradise and I had yet to feel unsafe on its streets or in its parks. In fact, I preferred strolling through Central Park in the dark and the cold. It was my favorite route home at 10:30 or 11, after an evening at the theater or one of those happy hours with someone you're gradually getting to know that begin at 5:15 and end six hours later. After about 9 p.m., the tourists and cyclists clear out, so it was usually just me, the occasional runner, a few dog walkers, and the gorgeous raccoons, who I view as more like rabbits than rodents. At certain points along the way, I've walked backwards to stare at the bright lights of the Midtown skyline, thrilled to have the greatest space in the supposedly greatest city all to myself for a change.

Two minutes into the mission, right when I was about to get my jog on, an NYPD van appeared in the distance. It stopped for a moment, slowly rounded a corner, heading toward me, eventually pulling up alongside me, and *those* bright lights hurt my eyes. As I tried getting out of its way, the passenger-seat cop rolled down his window and looked me in the eye. This whole episode could have ended differently if they, either one, hadn't been smirking. Years later, during another three-day weekend, on one of the *hottest* nights of the year, when a friend and I lounged on a bench by a duck pond in a different city park, another NYPD officer pulled his van onto the grass beside us and cordially conveyed that the park had officially closed hours earlier. We said sorry, he said no problem, we got up and out, and the interaction was eventful for nobody.

"Hi, do you know where you are?"

How's that for a hello, and what's next? How many fingers am I holding up? Can you tell me what day of the week it is? Who is the president of the United States? Now let's try to settle this once and for all—do you think it's really *better to have loved and lost than to never have loved at all?*

I immediately disliked him. Ditto with his driver. They didn't look billy-club dangerous as much as a little too excited about the sheer act of wearing those uniforms.

"What do you mean?" I asked.

"I don't think you know where you are."

"I'm near the Columbus Circle end of Central Park."

"Do you come here often?" This *would* be the cop I get.

"Yes."

"What if something happened to you and you needed to use one of those emergency call boxes?"

"Oh, I wasn't thinking about that, I was thinking about walking out of the park over there so I can get home."

"I know you weren't thinking about that. And if something *had* happened, we wouldn't know where to find you and would have had to search behind those rocks."

Huh?

"What's your point?"

I've received astonished reactions from many, but this was one for the blogs, if I'd had the wherewithal to keep up with one that winter. The things we're able to do with our facial muscles and eyeballs.

"The park is closed between 1 a.m. and 6 a.m."

"Well, I didn't know. So why didn't you just say that right off the bat?"

There it was. *His* breaking point. We all have more than one.

He asked for my ID. Couldn't imagine what he wanted with it, but I didn't want to be difficult, so I pulled it out and handed it over.

His driver put the van in reverse and parked it a few feet away from me. I watched them analyze my New York State ID card, taking no small comfort in the conviction that they were looking at what most would agree is my second-best government-issued ID photo (featuring that timeless Iron Lady facing the firing squad pose) on record. Passenger Cop produced a phone and called someone else, studying my ID as he snitched, while Driver Cop stared me down through the windshield. Twenty seconds later, Driver Cop looked down and away. Iron Ladies must never start staring contests, but it's our incontrovertible duty to win them.

I wasn't angry with these cops or the frigid windchill or the sub-par overnight subway service. I was angry with myself and who I still hadn't completely become. I was mad at the headspace I was in, previous headspaces, and decisions these headspaces had led me to make. I was mad about certain roles I had allowed myself to play in the past and roles I continued to reprise into the present, like the one involving the dispiriting multi-year "friendship" I had with the person whose home I had just left.

This was around the time when I was more hell-bent on solidifying the segue from my olden-days self to modern-times me. In the olden days, I was shyer and more deferential, as callow as they come. I didn't voluntarily contribute to classroom discussions, even if the reticence could have put me at risk of getting a slightly lower grade. I let people I had regular contact with mispronounce my name and offered to help those I barely knew move into new apartments. I went along and stayed silent, or acted like everything was OK, when I shouldn't have. I wanted to be fearless, but in a noble way. I had been transitioning from someone who let too many people have their way with her to someone who lets very few get past Stage One of any attempt to. (Some transformations take place over a series of small moments that don't seem to matter until we look back on them.) Every so often, this years-long process felt like an out-of-body experience. I became an outsider in my own life when it came to breaking into and getting to know my newer, updated self. I said and did things I didn't know I had in me, and some may have gotten caught in the cross-fire of my making up for lost time—such as a couple of bored and hapless Central Park Precinct officers who found themselves in the wrong place on the wrong night with the wrong tough-broad-in-training.

***

Yap, yap, yap. Passenger Cop and that phone. What did he have to talk about for so long? Maybe he was just pretending to be on the phone. I've done that. I dug around in my bag for a book and leaned the front of my body against the front of the van, where the temperature was warmer, resting my elbows on the hood as I tried reading a few paragraphs in the light of the low beams, which were pretty high up since I got the unit that was too high-post to roll in a sedan. I couldn't concentrate.

Not long after he jumped off his call, Passenger Cop reached his arm out of his window to return my ID and pass me a pink slip.

"Here's your summons," he said. "You can report to the courthouse on April 4."

What's a summons have to do with me? And I can report or I'm required to report?

"That's my dad's birthday. I'll see if I can make it." (My dad and I hadn't lived in the same metro area in years.)

He raised his eyebrows. There was a twinkle in his eyes as they reinvestigated mine. According to the lines of his lower face, he fought back a smile. Maybe he has an unruly mother, daughter, niece, or sister whom he adores to pieces. For a moment, I felt appreciated, possibly even somewhat seen.

As they began to drive off into the darkness, I looked down at the slip, confused about what came next. No longer in the headlights, I squinted at the scrawls on the ticket and saw April 1, not April 4. I walked along the passenger side of the slowly crawling van, asking why they did this to me. He said it was for being in the park after hours. Midway through my response, he got distracted by something up ahead. Now we had another young woman in the headlights, tottering through the park on high heels, the way I would walk in stilettos, which is why I don't wear them. Passenger Cop interrupted me and pointed at her. "We have to stop this person," he said.

I followed and stood a little ways back while both officers exited the parked van to question the drunk woman who said she was trying to get to Staten Island. As they spoke with her, Passenger Cop turned his head in my direction and did a fake double-take about my still being there.

"You can go now, ma'am," he said, sternly. No more Mr. Lax Cop.

"This ticket is ridiculous. You get back on that phone, call whoever it was you were talking to earlier, and get it reversed."

He said if I thought it was unjust, I'd have to tell it to the judge.

"So I might have to miss a day of work for this?!" Now I had the drunk's attention. "I'm sorry for being here after hours, but something like this only warrants a warning. I get that you're a prick on a power trip, but shouldn't you be going after rapists and murderers instead of people like me?"

I'm a crier. I cry at commercials about suffering children or animals. I cried after the Richards sisters got into an epic fight in the back of a limo on season one of *The Real Housewives of Beverly Hills*. I cry when I've been defeated or betrayed. I cry when I realize I made a big mistake or hurt someone. I cry when I conquered something huge that I worked hard for. I cry when I hear stories about how law enforcement has treated people with a darker skin color than mine. Like most things that feel natural, my crying is no big deal to me. But I can't handle seeing anyone else cry. I have a hard time witnessing another person drop his head and look close to tearing up, even when it's *not* because of something I said or did, even when it's law enforcement. On this night, remorse was in the air, there was a sanctity to our strife. Passenger Cop saw my struggle, my side. And I saw his. You read and know of so many stories about cops harassing people and getting away with it. This could be the only story you'll read about someone single-handedly harassing a cop and kind of getting away with it. I fought the law and there isn't anybody who won.

***

After more than a year of temp work, I found a new full-time position in my field. On the first day, I spent an under-caffeinated morning in HR, learning the intricacies of my new benefits plan. A nosy question on one form asked, "Do you have any pending criminal action against you?" *No*, I began to check off, *of course not. I ain't no thug.*

But, damn, am I? I thought, as unpleasant details from that pre-dawn run-in started coming back to me. *I'll never do a cop wrong again* (this was something I told myself before Ferguson and a lot of other police brutality tragedies that later followed in other parts of the country). Yes, I was flailing away from my more passive past, but the opposite extreme didn't work either.

A footnote[1] about how any failure to fully disclose would result in my immediate termination intimidated me enough to ask my new employer whether the pink slip counted. To avoid losing it and for show-and-tell purposes, mainly for the show and tell, I often kept it on or near me, thus was able to pull it out for the benefits coordinator in the blink of an eye. She held it close to her face, gaping at it before walking out of her office into the hallway and

---

[1] Or small print, or a parenthetical, or whatever.

central cubicle area, where a few of her colleagues milled around.

"Where is this brave woman who was in the park in the middle of the night?" someone bellowed directly behind me. Here came an assertive HR supervisor, holding the ticket, smiling down at me with delight. This made her day, I just knew it.

"Huh? Oh, that's me."

The benefits coordinator stood behind her. Incredulous giggling preceded incredulous silence. The supervisor said I had no obligation to report since I hadn't been fingerprinted.

So it's *fingerprinting* that can potentially unseat you. Very good to know for future reference, with the kind of future I could have coming if I didn't figure out how to meet my past and my present halfway.

***

April Fool's Day 2008:

The C train carted me down to the New York County Criminal Court building in Lower Manhattan. I wore a pinstriped suit and brought a copy of my résumé. After interminable morning rush-hour subway delays, I arrived at the courthouse 30 minutes late and stood in an hourlong line to await my courtroom assignment. Maddie (*remember her?*) was shocked I wasn't arrested. She mentioned she might want to come to court with me—for entertainment purposes, she made sure to make clear. In the spring of 2008, I still wasn't always great with saying goodbye to who or what had become familiar, so I ended up keeping her in my social circle for another four years. I would someday discover (as some people, and not just those two cops, may have discovered with me) that finally letting go of those who have brought little more than exasperation and grief into your life, as kindly as possible, has medicinal properties.

Courtroom 2, packed with people charged with public urination, was where they dealt with me and my kind. Every now and then, somebody would get called up to the front for reckless driving or an open-container violation, but it was the urinators who stole the show. I was the only person in a suit and one of the only women.

"Today, I am a lucky, *lucky* man," a beaming urinator sang as he glided out of the room, post-pardon.

I sure wouldn't want a public urination conviction on my record either, and wondered how he got out of it, again as a future reference thing, since I couldn't hear much from the middle of the airy room. I liked this crowd. The whole scene beat another day at the office, that's for sure. The upside to often feeling like you don't really belong anywhere is more than occasionally feeling like you belong everywhere, and I was dying to know what a few of these fine characters were up to after court that afternoon or evening.

Did I stand before a judge? Yes and no. Not in the recognizable, glamorous, scandalous sense. I stood before an assortment of delegates who took care of business. A couple of bailiffs, a stenographer, a dude standing at the side of each defendant, whispering procedural information into his or her (mostly his) ear. The bailiff who called out my name and my charge butchered my last name. I loudly corrected her once I reached the front of the room. An old man sat on a slightly elevated platform a few feet away, as if waiting to get his shoes shined. I think this was the judge. He didn't say a word to me, but periodically consulted with another random person sitting southeast of him.

Much like HR, the Courtroom 2 staff got a kick out of me and my charge. Once I was called forward, the Defendant Whisperer explained it would be recommended for dismissal and, in six months, the dismissal would become official. After I signed and dated a form, they thanked and released me.

"Where do I go now?" I asked, thinking there must at least be more paperwork involved. I was there to hold myself accountable—and as far as accountability went, this wasn't that bad. I'd rather pay a $50 fine than have to live with the memory of the crushed expression on Passenger Cop's face for the rest of my days.[2]

---

[2] I understand how lucky I am that these were the police officers I crossed paths with that night; and know that this encounter could have ended very differently, especially in that era before the ubiquity of iPhones.

"Home," they said with sympathetic, goofy, grins.

"Do I have to come back in six months?"

I didn't. An April Fool's Day that felt more like Easter morning! I stepped out into the sunlight, free at last—or free for then. Lady Justice, although I wish you worked longer hours, I do love when you are served. Justice is balance, balance is justice, and mastering that concept (most of the time) has set me free for good.

RUBBER BANDS FROM PUERTO RICO

Somebody stole my wallet in San Juan.

Eventually.

After I dropped it.

Standing and sweating in a short line, waiting for my Cuban sandwich ("the best *Cubano* in Condado," the deli cashier promised) to get wrapped up and ready to go, digging around in my bag for that huge clutch purse of a wallet (as long and wide as many *Cubanos* themselves) to check whether I had any bills smaller than a fifty. That's where I was and how I stood when I knew, beyond a shadow of a doubt, something was missing. It's not one of the better positions to be in when you're sidelined with an emergency involving much of the money to your name: (1) sweaty; (2) starving; (3) your skin tender from a possible sunburn even though you pancaked the white SPF cream on like clown makeup; (4) while one of your favorite foods is tantalizingly prepared directly in front of you; (5) on an island where, at the time and largely thanks to *Sesame Street*, you're able to speak and understand about two dozen words of the native tongue, eight (*ocho*) of those words being *hola, adios, gracias, agua, leche, feliz, Navidad,* and *Cubano.*

For days afterwards, every time my phone rang with a number steeped in mystery, I answered right away, so unlike me, to make myself available for breaking news—pickup/drop-off information, an apologetic explanation for having taken so long with the outreach, or whatever else the bearer of great news cared to share. I was sure someone would give back what was mine because it's happened for me before, two other times, with two other wallets. The first time was in the Metropolitan Museum of Art when I was in New York as a visitor, waiting for a friend to get off from work. A security guard returned it to Lost and Found within 20 minutes of my having left it behind, before I made it out of the museum. The second time, I was a novice New Yorker, on the subway coming home from the Chelsea T.J. Maxx. The finder diligently tracked me down using my former debit card. We met up at her boyfriend's Lower Manhattan lounge, where she returned the wallet, offered me a drink on the house, and unsanctimoniously encouraged me to return the favor if ever in a future position to do so. Most New Yorkers, the natives and those who have gone the expat route, aren't callous when it counts, unless they work in finance or real estate.

The painfully humid morning after my third time, I was too agitated to lie down. My phone and I sat upright on a chaise lounge facing the Atlantic Ocean. Although the beach no longer seemed that spectacular, pacing back and forth in my air-conditioned budget hotel room had turned intolerable. I assumed the outdoor air would be cooler by the water but it still sweltered. I just couldn't catch a breeze. I also somehow forgot to pack sunglasses for this week at the beach, and there was no nearby opportunity for any of the simple, sought-after sort of shadiness the good people of this galaxy don't get enough of.

An unidentifiable incoming call interrupted one of my outgoing calls! Here comes my money back, I got my money back, *viva* my money back!

My primary-care physician wanted to confirm the appointment for a physical I had in a few days. *What appointment?* I thought before telling her we'd better reschedule, not letting on that all was amiss, that I couldn't remember whether my health insurance cards were in that stolen wallet too. I didn't mention I was in the Caribbean or give her any reason to suspect I wasn't just another overbooked city girl, hectically but skillfully juggling extracurricular niceties in between her bookends of the professional and the personal. Making an appointment with an internist for a routine check-up is such a mundane way to spend a few minutes. How far in advance had I scheduled it, and had I called from my apartment or my office? It sounds like a line I would have later crossed off a to-do list, the ones I still hand-write on the back of junk-mail letters and envelopes. Early- to mid-crisis, vivid recollections of the mundane become enviably exotic, although you can't allow yourself to get distracted by too many of them if you want another invitation to that faraway land someday.

***

One week later, back in the City That Has Always Returned What I Drop, I pulled a hefty letter-sized envelope with a San Juan postmark, and no return address, out of my mailbox. The sender inked my middle initial in between my two real names and hermetically sealed the back of the envelope with scotch tape. I, too, am usually that neurotic with the packaging of outgoing mail and appreciated the meticulousness. Kindred spirits have ways of popping up when you least expect them to.

It had to have been the guy sitting across from and behind me on the virtually empty #21 bus, on the way back to Condado Beach from the Bacardi rum distillery. We took stock of each other as he walked past me after boarding, part-sinner-part-saint vibes in both sets of eyes and energies. I couldn't get a great read on him and he might have thought the same about me. We may have been loosely but courteously acquainted in a past life, and there's something unsettling about an unaccountably deep recognition that doesn't necessarily have anything to do with an out-and-out attraction.

After I jumped up to ring the bell across the aisle (of course, the bell by my own seat didn't work), the wallet must have tumbled out of my oversized, overstuffed, unzipped, brightly colored (island-chic) cloth bag onto the empty seat right in front of him, right before I tumbled out of the almost-empty bus. I have always pictured him heading home to a small, humid, dimly lit living space and pouring himself a cold drink before sitting down to slowly sift through it all, item by item, deciding what each of us really needed the most.

While he busied himself with that, I might have already been down at the city bus terminal, still supposing there was a possibility of filing a missing property report. "*Americano*," the only English-speaking bus driver on site summed me up, shaking his head at an off-duty colleague who had, minutes earlier, tried telling me I had no prayer, in Spanish. The bilingual one accepted a sheet of paper with my name and phone number carefully written on it. The unilingual one settled into his place at a communal table and began eating his dinner, continuing to react in Spanish, mostly to the other off-duty drivers. His hot meal smelled divine and reminded me that I never did sample that *Cubano*. When I'd told the Condado deli cashier I needed to take off sooner than planned, on account of having just left my wallet on a non-tourist-area-bound bus, he didn't hand over the almost-ready-to-serve sandwich, on the house, as a mercy meal. He nourished me with the following nugget: "You got a big problem."[3]

***

That little bandit from the back of the bus held onto my cash and coins, the book of stamps I'd bought earlier in the day of the theft to mail a postcard, and the wallet itself.

---

[3] This was years before Hurricane Maria upended lives and livelihoods on this island.

Everything else, he sent back home—the cards, the checkbook, the crumpled-up receipts from a South Harlem Rite Aid and the Old San Juan post office where I bought the stamps; the notes to myself about future errands to run and gift registry tracking numbers for weddings and baby showers. For the first time in a while, I'd had a lot of cash in my wallet. If those $50 bills helped release him (or a person he loves more than his island, more than our country) from an untenable position, my two days of pacing and panic were worth it. I'm a Libra and a native midwesterner, so I'm glad to have helped. I'd rather be a healer than a hater. That's the attitude I have today. While still on his island, I fantasized about having a mob boss contact who knew he owed me something and could put a couple of his more ruthless associates on a plane within an hour of receiving my call.

It's usually so black and white. People who find wallets either return them without rewarding themselves with prize money *or* they keep it all and forget about the person they dicked over. But who knew the world of wallet theft was like everything else? There's an impish fuzzy zone. Someone can steal all the money you have on you and still be a considerate person at the end of the day, can still feel bad about doing it. Had this one always meant to return what was of no use to him? Or did he find something during his contents investigation that changed his mind? He might have peeked at the scribblings in my checkbook register, seen how much rent I paid, and felt sorry for me. After flipping through the ID card photos and remembering me from the bus, even in the absence of a Spanish sur-name, he may have thought I was at least part Nuyorican, in town from the Big Apple to get more in touch with my roots. That's what pretty much everyone else down there seemed to think I was doing. I ran into a guy from Brooklyn who was in the middle of such a lofty pilgrimage with his elderly mother, revisiting their family's old haunts, taking note of all the updates. He, who had been born in San Juan, looked satisfied, like he got what he came for. She looked distressed and ready to go home, unsure of which direction to turn toward.

As miserable as I was, I felt comfortable on this island, in this community. My misery gained some unexpected company. Lots of these people looked like me. I could blend right in, such a relief and a release. I've stood out in most environments I've been in. My dad, my brother, and I are the only Blacks, and the only non-whites, in the family I grew up and spent time with. I spent my tween and teen years in a nearly all-white suburb that one company's website has named the fourth least diverse city in the country (as in the *entire United States*—this wasn't a regional ranking), and lived on a mostly white (aside from the cler-ical, technical, service, and maintenance staff) college cam-pus before moving to Boston, a city that tends to receive its darker-skinned residents like an HPV diagnosis. I'm not the only mixed-race person with a long history of getting mistaken for Puerto Rican, Dominican, Mexican, Colom-bian, Hawaiian, and so on. In San Juan, tourists asked me for directions; locals treated me as a local, nothing out of place until they realized I could only speak *Sesame Street* Spanish.

In Puerto Rico and outside of Puerto Rico, it plays out like this: someone with my general features or skin tone will notice and benignly, meaningfully, fairly animatedly, focus on my face for five to 10 seconds before stepping forward. He or she will ask or tell me something succinct in rapid Spanish, often zeroing in on every segment of my face, not just the eyes, with vigilant eagerness. This is all a test, only a test. One I'm set up to fail. I smile and shake my head and we default to English, unless the tester doesn't know English, which adds a layer of politely silent sadness to our personal space, as the link-at-first-sight spark begins to die down. All of this happened with the Brooklyn tourist and his mom. I couldn't cooperatively respond to his call, their Romance language, the one they thought we could share. He still invited me to join them on their joyride through the historic district, and I respectfully declined, but couldn't tell you why, in any language.

***

Here's another glimpse into the mind and values of the flawed fella I got: he tightly rubber-banded all the cards from my wallet into little separate stacks instead of tossing everything into the envelope without a system. Hello, Virgo?

His envelope was a pleasure to unpack. I had forgotten all I'd had in that wallet; and he knows more about me than many others in my midst do (the day and year I was born, that my organs will be up for grabs one day, how many weight fluctuations I've had since the age of 14). I'd kept the same student ID card all four years of college and in the years since then, an honor he made sure was only very briefly taken away from me. And all those rubber bands he sent over were a fringe benefit. Rubber bands that thick can be hard to come by, free of charge. I used them for years to securely bundle any opened packs of turkey bacon or other unresealable perishables in my fridge. They became additional souvenirs from that trip, along with the purse I rarely use, the set of leaky wooden coasters, and the broken earrings I wasn't allowed to return or exchange 24 hours after they were impulsively purchased.

If we became pen pals, the correspondence would not be drab. He could teach me more Spanish. I could try explaining what it's like to potentially deal with the kinds of biases Black people face *and* the preconceived notions that those who can pass as Hispanic might confront. I could describe the joy of shrieking, "No English, No English!" at a stranger I don't want to talk to who wants to talk to me. We'd comprehensively cover our good deeds, our bad deeds, our perfectionistic qualities that others dismiss as oddities. I'd get to the bottom of what he wanted with a beat-up, non-designer woman's wallet. It wasn't an eyesore but it was no looker. Was it for his mother or sister or wife; a lady friend he gets together with when no one else gives him what he needs when he needs it; a daughter, niece, or family friend's little girl to use as a dress-up prop? Or was it simply to safeguard his own money, some of which was mine?

My replacement wallet was a plain, brown DKNY classic that the person responsible for deeply igniting my racial consciousness, whose influence led me to start checking off the "Black/African-American" box instead of the "Black" *and* "White" (or "Mixed Race") boxes, gave me as a birthday gift when we were in our early twenties. I hadn't asked my friend Rhonda for a wallet, hadn't needed one, and didn't love this particular style. Having been stored away in a shoebox for roughly 10 years, ripe for regifting (although, as shameless of a regifter as I am, I was never able to bring myself to give it away to anyone else), after San Juan it became the most adaptable and cherishable wallet I ever used. Something I almost clung to. When the interior change purse frayed, I sealed the gaps with clear packing tape to keep the coins from slipping out, and came close to slipping back into pacing mode when the time finally came to toss out what I once used to help hold onto precious things.

Child's Pose

Yoga has really grown on me in that I usually no longer tense up at the sight or sound of the word "yoga." I've come a long way and, as of the most recent count, my personal evolutions have out-numbered the stagnations and devolutions, which has become my definition of success.

At least partly because of my yogic training, my posture has improved: **True**

An instructor has insisted that I have a real future as a yogi myself: **False**

Even so, I'm on the expressway to not tipping over (on or off the mat) as much: **True**

Immediately after doing yoga, I snack on yogurt, celery sticks, or bean sprouts: **False**

"Maharishi" quickly made my Most Beloved Words list (behind only persnickety, kerfuffle, dipsomaniac, meta, bespoke, *fakakta*, nonplussed, and *incroyable*): **True**

I enjoy moving slowly: **False**

My serenity reaches its peak when I'm barefoot: **True**

I've morphed into a significantly calmer member of society: **En Route to Becoming True**

Regarding that last point, many of those I'm not close to have described me as chill. All who truly know me understand that I'm a nervous wreck. An overriding goal of mine is to trigger just one loved one to characterize me— to my face, behind my back, posthumously, whatever—as "mellow." I'll also take "a cool cat."

My first set of adult yoga classes mirrored my memorable stint in childhood ballet. There, I held the title of being the only little girl who could never do a full split. I could have done without the repetitive drills, loved the pink tutus and soft slippers (the next best thing to bare feet), and adored my teacher, Miss Libby. She adored me back. As much as I underperformed, she never treated me like I was anything less than a gifted dancer with an inimitable star quality. I remember all five of the basic positions, feet and arms, and continue to regularly run through them, along with the pliés and pirouettes. While chopping onions or waiting to cross a busy street, I've been known to find my feet, still occasionally swathed in a now-larger and thicker pair of pink flats, falling into fourth or fifth position.

With ballet, burning out early or not having a reputation as a quick study didn't bother me. It was light and playful, something my mom and I thought could be cute. Yoga's different. I wanted to be outstanding at (not just improve on) it. Anyone claiming not to have something they wish they were great at, but aren't great at, no matter how much effort they've expended, either has no imagination, no self-awareness, or is straight-up lying. How much better or worse would this world be if each of us could cherry-pick our own talents instead of having them foisted upon us?

***

That first group yoga class took place in an intimate setting of merely three other students, meaning I didn't have the option of bringing up the rear and hiding behind rows of other bodies. The session quickly dove downhill, but my instinct to dart out of the room's partially closed doors while everyone's heads were bowed and eyes were closed was easier thought out than carried out. My acute stress level? Off the charts. I had assumed a yoga lesson amounted to nothing more than deep stretching, breathing, chanting, lying in Child's Pose for the length of a proper catnap—not gym class. The instructor was all over me, pointing out my every lacking. Midway through class she walked down the short line of students as we struck our poses.

"Good," she praised #1.

"*Good*," to #2.

"Good," to #3.

"Better," she said to me, after a hella awkward pause. This was no Miss Libby and "early dismissal" were two words, when joined together like siblings, missing from her working vocabulary. This yogi who had come into my life could only be charmed by her fellow human pretzels, the ones whose bodies were like bendy straws, flexible enough to do splits or form positions that could qualify them for a circus act or a tournament of perverts. I pegged her as someone who rises with the Sun and courteously refuses meat and refined sugar, in between meditation sessions on the tops of hills. A lifestyle that fascinates me as much as it turns me off. The closest I've come to it is sitting in cafés that offer wheatgrass shots, buying accessories from almost every Eastern culture-themed store I've set foot in, and eating sushi. I've seen a yogi from my old neighborhood's flagship yoga center at the grocery store. She seemed to be a sushi nut as well and the realization of the shared interest/contents of our baskets once connected us in a checkout line. YOGA IS FOR EVERYBODY, a sign outside of her studio told it like I guess it could be.

After two or three more classes, I announced my retirement and donated my original, royal blue yoga mat to a friend. From what I could tell, nobody missed me. A few years later, I found myself missing *it* and the toning and fluidity yoga brought to my tense and rigid body. I practiced some of the moves at home a few times a week, while listening to music or watching TV. No mat, no New Age pretentions. Just long pants, solid floorboards, a decent amount of determination, and my multi-purpose bed.

***

When I decided to give public yoga another chance, five years after disowning it, I was open to a fresh start, a new and better chapter of my personal book (a dramedy) of Zen. My Zen is zany and I found a new mat in a shade of purple that is slightly more reflective of this reality. I managed to wake up early enough on a Saturday morning to make it to a free hourlong yoga class at a local branch of the New York Public Library. Knowing my bare feet would be on display, I had painted my toenails pink because I needed to save some face about my feet. Since my last yoga class, I'd picked up a medium-sized scar on the top of my left foot after having spilled half a pot of scalding water on it. The doctor dubbed it a deep second-degree burn, one step below a mild third-degree burn. He (who subbed for my real and nicer doctor while she was out on maternity leave) told me I'd be "scarred for life," and wasn't wrong. A former boss gave me a tiny jar of scar-minimizing cream that members of the elite circles supposedly swear by. It didn't work, but nobody in my subsequent yoga classes seemed to care about or notice this enlarged and discolored beauty mark, as the very idea of doing yoga clearly sent them into quite a zone. During and after each move, most of them looked euphoric, as if they'd just popped a molly, while I learned how long I could hold back cusses and screams.

As far as I know, I don't own yoga pants and (much like with "boyfriend jeans" or "mom jeans") don't totally understand what they are, no matter how many times I see them or have them explained to me. I had a drawer half-full of Capri sweatpants I wore to bed, to lounge around in, and when I ran errands. These were the pants I wore to yoga. I debated whether to buy a newer, voguer, more form-fitting outfit for my revival class. The Nays/Why Would I Want to Do Thats? won by a landslide that was crooked but final. A few days later, I read a soft-hitting piece of online journalism about a popular yoga pants retailer having to recall 17 percent of the pants (costing "roughly $100" apiece!) it sold within a one-week period because they'd been unknowingly see-through. Here's the statement a brand spokesperson released: "We want you to Down Dog and Crow with confidence and we felt these pants didn't measure up" (and one more game I've been so behind on, I've actually been ahead).

Pulling my pants on with pride, I tried hyping myself up for this big comeback class. Immediately after removing my mint-condition mat from the plastic wrapping, I ruined its carrying harness and gave up on trying to fix it. Patience is something I was working on, not a quality I already seamlessly brought to the table, and too much playing around with the straps and buckles would have made me late. I shoved the loosely rolled-up mat under my arm and walked across Morningside Park to the host library branch, whose front doors were still locked. A small group of elementary school-aged kids waited with me, eager to get inside, playing a spirited game of tag on the sidewalk to kill time. The yoga class was held on the children's floor, so when the doors opened at 10 a.m., we all headed up the stairs in the same direction.

A few minutes after I signed and dated a waiver, the instructor kicked off our three-person class. More intimacy, but everyone in the room was likable and three is a very spiritual number. The other two students were semi-beginners too, friendly, curvy ladies who had dabbled with yoga in the past and didn't hanker for anything too convoluted. We had no aspirations to advance to the intermediate level or whichever stage it is that pressures you into doing headstands and metamorphosing into a stationary gymnast. I've seen photos of people on yoga websites doing things with their bodies that drive home how I'm better off training for marathons, namely the ones that don't overly involve running.

The instructor said this would be a Hatha Yoga class, focusing on breathing and holding the various poses, instead of the faster-paced and more aerobic Vinyasa Yoga which is the harried hand I must have been dealt years earlier. I'd come to the right place. Yogi 2.0 didn't reach out and touch people's backs, hips, and stomachs without consent. She didn't encourage perfection, much less expect it. She let us be us. We had an instructor, not an inspector who closely studied how many inches our backs bridged off the floor or how ideal of an angle our arms formed during a warrior pose. In ballet, it was spotting—my pint-sized classmates and I would line up to, one by one, take on the task of trying to smoothly and rapidly twirl across the floor in a straight line, by keeping our eyes focused on the same specific spot. In yoga, it's poses like Downward-Facing Dog. I effortlessly master and find comfort in undertakings that a number of beginners have said they find the most difficult. Figuring out so many of the basics is what has consistently thrown me.

Surrounded by carts of long and thin colorfully covered books, Dr. Seuss hats, stuffed animals, building blocks, and miniature chairs, I time-traveled back to a more familiar and less sweaty place (to the 1980s, to be exact), when I hung out in public library children's rooms week after week. I went to the library when I was happy, when I was sad, when I was bored—libraries and books were my earliest forms of self-medication. Mindfully balancing, Sun Saluting, and lying down in this room more than two decades later reminded me who and what is underneath all the efficiency, stamina, and wisecracks that have rounded out my adult persona. I felt lighter, the tension was tempered, as I re-became the kid who skipped into children's rooms, fondling and forking over her treasured library card, considering it part privilege, part right. I continued to relax as I thought of the towering stacks of books I checked out, the overdue fines I racked up, and the summer reading programs that accepted and rewarded the first book reviews I ever drafted. I earned my family tickets to Cleveland Indians baseball games through those summer reading programs I outperformed in. Bleacher seats, but every single one of those ballgames was glorious and allowed me to bring home some bacon of my own.

Always the unapologetic, compulsive reader, going to the library was part of a routine, like leaving for school in the morning or brushing your teeth before bedtime. Books and magazines exposed me to a larger world I wanted in on. I loved Amelia Bedelia and Ramona Quimby but wished I could be more like Cam Jansen and the "bossy" founder of *The Baby-Sitters Club*.[4] Books and magazines made me want to live in different cities and have stellar stories to bring back from trips to other continents, go out with boys who rode motorcycles, and make a career out of bouncing back from unforeseen disappointments, constantly trying new things, even things I doubted I'd be any good at. As I stepped out of the library's front doors at the end of that yoga class, I looked at my phone and saw the time was 11:11 a.m. The luckiest minute of the day, as some believe, and the official minute of my birth. I normally make a wish or the sign of the cross whenever I see all four of those numbers lined up, but didn't feel the need to then, some luck had kicked in. I'd walked into that yoga room for some Zen and I got it.

I prefer libraries to bookstores, the same way I prefer oceans to swimming pools. You can have $23 in your bank account and still feel loaded in a library. The stores may keep longer hours and don't carry books that reek of cigarette smoke, but I've never been in one that felt like a church or the Statue of Liberty, convincingly welcoming to all walks of life and states of minds. Come Election Day,

---

[4] From what I remember, *The Baby-Sitters Club* series (featuring all of one Black main character and all of one Asian main character) represented some of the most diverse children's/young adult books I had been introduced to back in my day.

there are no voting booths set up in a bookstore. Nobody's mansion and no prison includes a solemn space referred to as "the bookstore." Public yoga isn't for everyone but public libraries still are.

***

Rather than spending half the day in bed and repositioning myself every 45 minutes, I returned to class the following Saturday morning to practice the hell out of Hungover Yoga. Hungover Yoga involves a good deal of squinting, stumbling, and deeming yourself a martyr for deciding against sleeping it off on a day off. The children's room was packed with close to 10 yoga students and I finally got what I asked for—a row of people to hide behind. It was a more challenging class than the week before and not just because I was coming off a rough night. Thank God these library sessions were free. I couldn't see a lot of what the instructor demonstrated up front, but not to worry; she, the Miss Libby of our time, made her rounds and gently tried helping me loosen up, to no avail. We smirked at each other before she moved on. "Thank you for your practice," she purred from her seated position once the hour was up, less than five minutes before I hightailed it into a Dunkin' Donuts across the street to celebrate.

There are people who deliberately do 90 consecutive minutes of this, with the heat turned all the way up, without reparations.

You bet I took a four-week hiatus after that class. I spent some of that time buying new Capri sweats, breathing deeply, and eating sushi, devoting much of one lunch break to a free exhibit at New York Public Library headquarters that covered the history of the lunch break in New York. So meta! I've hid out and decompressed in public library reading rooms during many lunch breaks, leaving these peaceful buildings more centered and healed than when I came in.

During my Saturday morning comeback the following month, I struggled with poses that hadn't given me trouble before. I'd lost strength and muscle during my time away and was more concerned about the strength. One person rolled up his mat and left 10 minutes before class adjourned. I understood the impulse and the value of defying it. All the cold water I would chug and iced coffee I would suck down after completing the challenge I'd started would be two of my rewards. Yoga is as much of a like-dislike relationship as many of my most meaningful long-term relationships have been. The kind of relationship you eventually realize you won't completely sever, no matter how tempting the thought of it might be during certain heated, elongated moments. My only beef with public libraries is that they're not open 24 hours.

The next Saturday morning, I was out of town. I practiced Tree Poses and Sun Salutations in my hotel room, overlooking a parking lot. (After discovering that another local branch library offered yoga on Thursday nights, I thought about taking my practice primetime. Each time

Thursday night rolled around, it was too hot out, I needed an evening of unstructured downtime, or I suddenly developed a fanaticism about scrubbing down every crevice of my fridge.) The Saturday morning after that, I visited an optometrist, wearing pants I've worn to yoga, feeling quite limber in them, to update a prescription for my reading glasses. I had a lot of new library books on my nightstand. Afterwards, I came home and performed a string of Sun Salutations, pliés, and jumping jacks, figuring I could shuffle back into the semi-sublime at a branch library whenever the urge overtook me, without owing anyone anything.[5]

It wasn't long after that when the next mass solicitation email from the New York Public Library's fundraising committee landed in my inbox. I didn't have the heart to ignore it. Between the yoga and other classes I've almost flocked to (Jewelry making! Adult coloring! Chess! Microsoft Excel!), the number of books and DVDs I've checked out (saving me incalculable amounts of money and space), and the free internet I took advantage of (in the pre-iPhone years) before my salary was middle class enough to get high-speed service in my home, the least I could do was send as much as I could afford over to one of my soundest sources of spiritual solace.

Namaste.

---

[5] Coronavirus-related update: as of this writing, it's hard to say whether the New York Public Library will ever offer free in-person yoga classes again.

ACCOMMODATIONS

When my dad first saw the South Harlem studio apartment I used to live in, he, without hesitation, put it all on the (thrift-store) table: "This is a nice apartment—for New York. Anywhere else it'd be a slum." An observation that couldn't have been more on the money, but he never laid eyes on my first New York City bachelorette pad. Half a decade earlier, I had moved into town knowing remarkably little about what I was getting myself into other than that a tarot card-reading Cambridge, Massachusetts, psychic had once forewarned that New York was my destiny, where things would begin to happen for me. A corollary to the prophecy (at least on my end) was the expectation that, whenever I did manage to roll into residency, I would always and only live in Manhattan, the alpha borough, whose streets were as goldenly grimy as those who gallivanted all over them.

I moved to New York at 25 years old, showing up (at the Port Authority terminal, a stone's throw from Times Square, on a Greyhound bus) with not much more than a huge duffel bag and an overstuffed handbag. It was springtime; Cinco de Mayo was my first day at the first salaried, career-track job I ever held. I stayed with a cousin in Chelsea for a little more than two months while searching for my own spot, and already had a local collection of friends and acquaintances I had gone to school with in place. I remember going out my first night as a resident, quite certain my adulthood years were kicking off in earnest, convinced I was on the cutting edge of something monumental. I just had to find some dope-ass new living quarters.

***

The first New York apartment I rented sits in the Astoria section of Queens, the borough from which Rhonda, my most glamorous ride-or-die friend (who has never lived in Miami but will mass-email a Miami-based photo of her and Lady Gaga sitting backstage before or after a concert), hails. When the broker showed me the exceptionally small but affordable space, it seemed decent enough, which I guess is all that matters when you were raised middle class, earn a salary that doesn't amount to much more than the babysitting money you pulled in during high school, self-identify as a free spirit, and have yet to learn anything useful about apartment hunting in New York. Before signing the lease, I got to meet the soon-to-be departing tenants, an attractive young couple who said they hadn't had any problems there. In fact, they seemed heartbroken about leaving. To this day, I'm convinced they were actors, earning a daily rate from the broker, the landlord, the city, or an even darker and more dangerous power.

There are two things, thus far, I haven't totally been able to get used to, no matter how many years have passed: my mother being dead and living in New York City. Nothing about living in New York has ever passed as normal to me, someone who is Midwest born and bred. After a brief stint in Michigan during my toddlerhood, I grew up in Cleveland, Ohio, home of the Rock-and-Roll Hall of Fame, Malley's Chocolates, American Greetings (which has been second only to Hallmark in terms of the world's largest greeting card producers), and the companies that first brought us Lip Smackers and ballpark mustard. As a teenager, I couldn't wait to break free from Middle America and only seriously considered non-midwestern colleges. In college and after college, I've gravitated toward midwesterners, whenever I'm lucky enough to find them. By my mid-twenties (after having lived in the South, New England, and the Mid-Atlantic region), I began to profoundly appreciate where I come from. By my late twenties, I became a Midwest supremacist. I pledge allegiance to the nasally accents, the winsome warmth, the ready smiles and over-apologizing, women over 30 referring to Express or the Limited as purveyors of "expensive clothes," people wearing hats to keep their ears warm instead of as a fashion statement. Whether I'm back in Cleveland, or in Indiana, Illinois, Wisconsin, and so on, I'm overtaken by the same serenity. I wouldn't mind raising a family of my own, dying, or reincarnating in the Midwest because I didn't relocate to New York City out of boredom, or because I'd dreamed of experiencing the "energy" or "excitement" I'd read about or seen on *Sex and the City* and *Seinfeld* episodes. When I got out of school, I wanted to work and start making a name for myself as an editor. New York was the first metro area that invited me to do so, on a full-time basis, with built-in health insurance and a retirement plan I hazily understood.

When I read *The Great Gatsby* in high school, I thought it was pretty good but it meant about as much to me as those well-meaning "Never Change!" directives we used to write in yearbooks; I had no context. It took, years later, two rereadings for me to realize that it's mostly about how midwesterners are the ones who can have the hardest time adapting to the New York State of Mind.

***

Astoria (a seven-letter word bearing a strong resemblance to "America"; that and this Queens neighborhood's proximity to my Rockefeller Center cubicle were two of its chief allures) and I did not get to enjoy so much as a honeymoon period. On Day One, after entering my itsy-bitsy new apartment by picking at what was left of the lock with the tip of my key, I learned I would need to buy and install my own toilet seat. Not long after that, the bathroom sink detached from the wall and crashed to the floor. "Well, you better sweep it all up, I wouldn't want you to cut yourself," was the guy from the landlord office's opening response.

In my student days, a number of my classmates studied with earplugs in libraries, coffee shops, and unoccupied classrooms. Made of foam and contouring to the host set of eardrums, they're surprisingly comfortable, pleasurable even, like floating inside of a cloud. In Astoria, I began sleeping with them firmly in place every night to block out the sounds of rodents scrambling through the walls and communicating with each other via high-pitched squeaks underneath the floorboards. When she stayed with me for a couple of days, I gave a visiting friend her own pair of earplugs before turning out the lights for the night. I explained they were simply to suppress the sounds of the street noise and early-morning pigeons on the windowsills, painting the option of wearing them as something of a luxury, the auditory equivalent of donning a silky eye mask, too embarrassed to admit what they were really meant to cover up. As I lounged in bed another night, a mammoth-sized cockroach (which many other locals would refer to as a waterbug; the first time you see one indoors, which this was, you're face to face with a creature out of science fiction) crawled up my comforter.

That year, the building's super was most super about ignoring my phone calls and standing me up. A neighbor told me she had taken the landlord's office to housing court, but nothing seemed to come from it. As a realist, my top priority became getting professionally established enough to no longer live low paycheck to low paycheck. On the warm-weather nights I returned to my Astoria hovel after another long, underpaid, thankless day as an editorial assistant, I liked to stick my head out of the window that formed a right angle with my kitchen sink and breathe in the fresh-ish air, resting my elbows on the sill, taking in my view of what must have been the Triborough Bridge, which looked lovely, all lit up when the sky turned black and the moon stayed white. I would gaze down onto the back porch of a house on a residential strip, where a young couple, no more than 10 years older than me, frequently hosted the most joyful of happy hours. Wine, appetizers, sparkling conversation, belly laughter. From my perch, the hosts came off as the most down-to-earth and emotionally satisfied members of any group they ever had over, and I couldn't wait to be one half of them someday, no matter what part of the country or world I lived in. They looked like newlyweds and newly minted homeowners, giving me something else to aspire to, a local template to work from, a refreshing contrast to my upstairs neighbors who maniacally laughed, stomped on their floor/my ceiling, playing Jimi Hendrix's "Hey Joe" ad nauseum into the wee hours. Although I would have preferred auto-replays of "Hey Jude" to "Hey Joe" ("I shot her!" the stompers overzealously screamed along with the tail end of the lyrics), their ruckus relaxed me more than the vermin serenades coming from inside the walls, which I prayed would turn into vermin suicides.

For years, back in Middle America, my friend Kristen lived in a beautiful apartment in a building about an eight-minute walk from the suburban street we grew up on. She paid something like $27/month for it and shared a balcony with her next-door neighbors, an older man who lived with his hot son. The dad baked and brought over fresh loaves of bread, which she said were delicious. My dad brings his neighbors tomatoes and cucumbers from his garden, while his neighbors bring him flowers, Christmas cookies, home-made *limoncello*, a plate of ribs straight off the grill. Here, Out East, I've had one neighbor leave an unsettling poem at my door and another bring me a liquor-tinged note read-ing: "*Madzi: What is your opinion? Please call me at 212-665-****. Fluoride is killing us.*"

New York, Boston, Washington, DC, North Caro-lina—although I've never lived more than about 600 miles away from home, so often has it seemed like much farther. New Yorkers tell me I have a midwestern accent. After hearing me talk for more than a few minutes, people out-side of New York have asked which part of Gotham I'm from. While walking through a room of Himalayan art at a midwestern museum, I find myself itching to get back to the six-floor Lower Manhattan museum that's entirely devoted to Himalayan art. In suburban Flyover State gro-cery stores, I've thought about how at least one person in a New York checkout line (long before the days when single-use plastic-bag bans went into effect) would have brought a reusable canvas bag and doubt that many would give much of a second glance to a woman wearing a *hijab*. When I spend Christmas in New York and need to buy a few last-minute grocery items at 9:10 p.m. on Christmas Eve, I have my pick of nearby stores to dash into. Back in my part of Cleveland, most places would have already shut down for the holiday; but the tranquility of those Middle American Christmas Eve streets (some years, blanketed with salvation-esque snow) better captures the essence of what that holy night commemorates. At a $20 all-you-can-eat seafood and sushi buffet in Manhattan, I've bragged about Kristen's and my favorite $7 buffet (which includes sushi and seafood) in a Middle American strip mall, before confessing that the quality of the fish in this pricier place is second to none I've had.

***

I signed the lease and moved into the South Harlem studio apartment I went on to rent for 12 years when I was in my late twenties. It was my first New York City apartment that provided some serious shelter from the tsunami. "Do you have a terrace?" a "lifelong New Yorker," who's only ever lived in the suburbs, once asked. There was no terrace, no dishwasher, no microwave, no silverware drawer, no bathroom towel rack, no medicine cabinet (just a cheap and thin mirror attached to the bathroom wall), no pretty window views. But this place was generally everything I dreamed my New York City crib would be when I was 25 and 26 and fantasizing about living in an apartment I wouldn't be obsessed with staying away from. It's where I did my best sulking, really taught myself how to cook, honed my hostessing skills, and drafted my first personal essay, concluding I'd sulk less if I wrote more (you are now reading the eighth or ninth big-picture revision of that first essay).

Outside of my email exchanges, day job duties, and personal journal entries, I barely wrote a paragraph in Astoria or while later living with roommates on the Upper West Side. After several years of moving every summer, within the same chaotic city, it's a major accomplishment to lay roots in the exact same spot of your own, no matter how shabby it may seem to visiting midwesterners. To not have to keep sending everyone your updated mailing address. To make a hobby out of gradually decorating a space you strove for. To have local shopkeepers offer you customized discounts and big smiles, alluding to how much they've missed you if you haven't walked through their door in a while. Memories of my twenties mostly revolve around how maddening it was to fight and flail for the slightest bit of stability, residential or otherwise. In my thirties, as everything else in every sphere of my life continued to change, this South Harlem studio apartment remained a constant. A trusty bomb shelter, even when I received the latest explosive news while hunkered down inside of it. Residential stability came first and the rest followed, taking its sweet time. Leaving that apartment after more than a decade, long after I outgrew it, for a bigger and bougie-er place farther uptown, where I live now, was much less emotionally taxing than I'd thought it would be.

I still usually sleep with earplugs in New York, and now it really is to mute all the noise seeping in from outside. I get them from Rite Aid (the drugstore that used to be the closest to my house in suburban Cleveland) instead of New York-based Duane Reade. Until it went out of business, I went out of my way to browse for books at the Michigan-based Borders chain instead of Barnes & Noble. I haven't ever had a sip of soda, diet or otherwise, only pop.

***

Just like in Astoria, in the South Harlem studio, I lived on the fifth floor and had a musically inclined upstairs neighbor, only this person performed his own music instead of blasting the music of others. I think I occasionally heard a live horn, but it was more commonly an acoustic guitar. What a delicacy to wake up to the smooth sounds of that strumming from above, which could come at any hour of the day.

Coming home to the studio one night, I saw a note taped to my next-door neighbor's door:

> Please turn your TV volume down a bit. It's
> really loud for your neighbors. Thank You!

What a civil way to call out a nuisance, I thought as I snatched the piece of paper off the door and brought it into my own unit. I figured the complaint had to be in reference to my latest hijinks and couldn't let the guy next door (who once offered to let me sleep on his family's couch after overhearing I'd locked myself out; who was sometimes so quiet

I forgot I had a next-door neighbor) take the fall. I was the loudest member of our corridor; it was me they wanted. The night before, I watched TV reruns until 2 a.m. to help put myself to sleep. An Emergency Broadcast System warning blared out at one point. That was a cause of the cacophony, what woke me back up after dozing off, what finally made me turn the noise off. If the strummer had been awake, picking at the guitar, I might not have needed the TV. But I also wouldn't have had the chance to take in that note, in all of its graciousness, and find renewed comfort in the perpetual possibility of stumbling into midwestern manners outside of the Midwest.

Loads of people move to New York and enjoy the good, bad, and utterly ugly for one to five years before throwing in the towel and moving back to their home regions, or a region more similar to it, on respectable terms. Which is something I threatened to do (i.e., by actively searching for jobs and brand-new beginnings in seemingly more tolerable locales, from Cleveland to Qatar) for years before realizing I didn't need to. I've lived in New York City longer than I've lived in any metro area since the age of 17, this strange and inspiring place where everyone's rushing off to get something done, avoiding the rookie mistake of assuming they'll have all the minutes in the world to make a dent in their short- and long-term hopes and dreams. Once you've kept your head above water in New York City long enough, it can often feel like you wouldn't be able to make it anywhere else for more than a matter of months.

***

Moments after landing at Cleveland's Hopkins Airport one afternoon, from wherever I lived at the time, my seatmate looked over at me and said, "You look like someone who's home." When I think of home, I think of the house I lived in and the street I lived on until I was 10 years old. This used to be a wonderful middle-class neighborhood, fewer than 10 miles west of downtown Cleveland. Now, every time I've driven by "the old house" when I'm in the area, it looks like a trap house, with the entire block looking like it's in on the trap game. In the 1980s, that house was my urban *château*. Maybe it was trappy while I lived there—if it was, I didn't pick up on it. That's where and when I was most at ease. The place where my grandmother and her sister held court (and me) before, during, and after boisterous extended family gatherings. The front yard where my oldest cousin tried teaching me how to do a cartwheel. The spacious front porch and the back balcony where our private view of the local Fourth of July fireworks was nothing short of stupendous. The backyard (with the fenced-in vegetable garden) where we sat on summer nights watching the airplanes make their descent into Hopkins, and where I played basketball with my dad (and also where someone eventually stole the basketball hoop that hung above our garage door). Even after overhearing that the house across the street got broken into and it was time to flee to the suburbs, I was kind of in my element over there.

Today, every time I'm in a car that's about to turn onto that street and slowly drive by "the old house," I hope to catch sight of at least one current occupant puttering around outside, preferably on her tree lawn, as the car slows down and I peer and ponder. "This is the house I grew up in," I plan on proudly saying after rolling down my passenger-side window. Then she'll smile and say something to the effect of, "Would you like to come inside and take a look around, to see what's changed?" before we pull over and accept the guided tour, the main tour guide being me.

***

I decided to check in on the old Astoria neighborhood eight years after the day I victoriously moved out and into a room five floors above a dive bar on the Upper West Side of Manhattan. I wanted to see if my old Queens apartment building was still standing; and to remind myself how far I'd crawled. Now that I've seen and soaked up more of it, I not only love Astoria, I'm thrilled to head into Queens for anything—Mets games, US Opens, lunch buffets and fabric stores in Jackson Heights, the Jamaica Avenue strip, root canal specialists in Rego Park. It's, hands down, my favorite outer borough, with its Middle American-like simplicity, lack of putting on too many airs, people who have the instinct to smile instead of the alternative.

As I got off at the 30th Avenue stop of the N train and walked toward one site of my ancient ruins, from a distance I saw commercial or community signage above my former building's main entrance. Finally, I thought, that dump has been condemned for residential use! The men from the landlord's office have been run into the ground after a well-attended public stoning, and now the property is used as a historical society or an indoor flea market. Turns out, the sign was for an organization whose office space was just downstairs from, off to one side of, the apartment building's front door. I don't know if it had been there while I was.

One of the best moves I made in my roaring twenties was to take tons of pictures of and with everyone. I didn't own an iron until I'd lived in New York for about five years. Didn't borrow one either; I had bigger problems to straighten out. Yet when I look through old photos from that period (most of which were taken with disposable cameras), none of my clothes look wrinkled. Neither do I, as grueling and aggravating as those years were. In the pictures, I'm glowing. Confused, broke, restless, often feeling like I was doing something big (or about to) even when I wasn't, still not considering it big enough. I haven't forgotten the subway rides down to the Village, the dives we wandered into, conversations and altercations, attempts to prepare for the years to come, if we were lucky enough to make it that far, as if we knew what we were doing. It was that vague brand of happiness, when you're happy without fully processing that you're happy. One or two steps short of having the time of my life, without realizing, until much later, that this era may have been my prime; and that primes can pass almost as fast as an NYC express train.

Climbing the Astoria building's front staircase, I figured I'd have to wait for an inmate to come in or out so I could slither inside and take a self-guided refresher tour. Not at all—the front door effortlessly swung open when I pushed it and sailed straight in, through the lobby, and into the elevator that still made disconcerting noises the whole way up. Everything was quiet, desolate, somewhat sinister. Nobody was in the lobby, on my old floor, or on any floor. This was a place where poor people lived. Out of all the places I lived when I was poor, this was the worst.

I walked down my former hallway and turned the corner toward 5E, to stand before and study the door for a few seconds before turning around to head down the closest set of stairs. It was so silent, I again hoped the entire operation was found guilty and financially deprived people weren't allowed to live there anymore, until I heard the sounds of elderly coughing and saw cracks of non-natural light coming from behind closed doors. I continued taking the stairs all the way down and walked out onto the street, through a side door that was still never locked, sick with survivor's guilt, but well enough to rush back to Home Sweet Harlem, where I fell into my bed, underneath an unthrowoutable comforter, each of which got their big starts in Astoria.

So Now I've Seen Paris

How better to ring in Valentine's Day than by landing in Paris to spend a week there by yourself? Every single gal's fantasy, *n'est-ce pas?* Paris is the city for couples, or at least a couple of people who really like each other. But none of the people I was willing to travel with were able and ready to jet off to France that February; and I wasn't about to let that hold me back. Right before leaving the US, I learned I would have no cell phone service—no calls, texts, or internet—so I was exceptionally by myself, assuming I would love it, as I usually crave alone time the way others crave chocolate.

Chocolate got in my face that whole week. And bread. My God, the white bread. Between the *patisseries, boulangeries, fromageries,* and the Rue Saint-Jacques, I found myself in the middle of my old richly illustrated French textbooks. In my high school French classes, I reigned supreme. On and around the real Rue Saint-Jacques, my VIP status needed a search-and-rescue operation. I was in my early thirties and the only person in my family who hadn't traipsed up and down the streets of Paris. My parents honeymooned there. My brother studied abroad there. Ours was not a clan that could afford European group vacations. Instead of France, the four of us road-tripped to Québec, which wasn't bad but wasn't this Paris I'd heard about since preschool. No place was, it seemed. If my not-easily-awed parents (while driving up Chicago's Lake Shore Drive, my mom once said, "You know, the Sears Tower really isn't that tall") revered it, that said something. "London is my favorite city," I announced at either 19 or 20, after my own little six-week study abroad adventure. "That's because you haven't seen Paris yet," my dad answered with an end-of-story confidence I didn't argue with.

Instead of a conventional hotel (which would have had a business center, even if the business center turned out to be one ramshackle computer, from which I could have sent and received personal emails), I stayed at an "exclusive guest house" in Montmartre, five or six units arranged around an inner courtyard with no identifying outdoor signage, at the foot of Sacré-Coeur. An acquaintance whose taste I trust stayed there a year earlier and recommended it. That's the only reason I slept solo in a place that required the week's payment in full, upfront, in cash. Very *Goodfellas*, but very clean, affordable, and a five-minute walk to the Anvers metro stop. When I booked the room, the co-owner, Renée, emailed that she and her man would be out of town my last day, leaving me home alone. Immediately after meeting her, I handed over hundreds of euros and made some Nespresso coffee in my freezing cold room, bracing myself for Round One of sightseeing.

In addition to the home alone thing, Renée and I had an email exchange about sneakers. My pink-and-gray New Balance running shoes. This would be a whirlwind sightseeing blitz, and I asked whether using these sneakers as my walking shoes would make me a sitting duck for the Parisian pickpockets the seasoned globetrotters in my social network wouldn't shut up about. I wanted to blend in as much as possible. According to Renée, everyone else would be wearing sneakers too. She stressed the greater importance of bringing a jacket with an inner pocket for my money. And that even children were trained thieves.

From the backseat window of the Peugeot that sped me to the 18th *arrondisement* from the incredible Charles de Gaulle Airport (where moving walkways seamlessly doubled as escalators—so exciting by 8 a.m. local time, after no sleep on the plane!), I could tell I was in trouble with the wardrobe I'd packed. Oh, how the running shoes would add to it. Every single pickpocket would show me up in the outfits department. The streets, all of them, were like a Stella McCartney runway show. The Parisians dress for errand-running or grabbing lunch with a friend the way I might dress for a banquet or a first meeting with Oprah. They put themselves together in a way I typically won't. With any given ensemble of mine, something will be off, whether it's a scuffed-up shoe, frayed socks, chipped nail polish, a hole in the inner thigh of my jeans. I will find a way to continue wearing or using many clothes, shoes, and handbags until they completely fall apart or lose their function. I carried a big, black, beloved Liz Claiborne tote for

15 years, finally throwing it out when all inner linings were ripped to shreds and no amount of heavy-duty stapling or binder-clipping could continue keeping the straps attached to the body of the bag itself. The French don't do this. I suspect the average living wage-earning American doesn't either.

In my late teens, my mom spent a few days in Paris, on her way home from a work-related trip to Spain. By herself, too. *Self-sufficiency is one of the most important qualities to have*, she told me at more than one point during my nurturing-without-mollycoddling upbringing. Paris was my mom's idea of heaven, as close as any metro area possibly could be. A big reward for those who could use one. She was a French teacher, which most likely helped. When you're in or just thinking about your heavenly haven, I'd imagine it's all the more blissful when you have the local language down. I used to help grade papers for her for allowance money, checking stacks of true-and-false and multiple-choice responses against an answer key. It was the kind of work that could get monotonous, but it gave us more time to chat or stay in each other's company. "Deshawn Davis got them all right," I would announce from the living room floor, while she sat on the couch reviewing the short-answer and essay sections. "How did Adriana Forman do?" she'd ask, and I'd search for Adriana's paperwork. When I found it, I sometimes graded it on the spot, to give her a solid answer right away, hoping as I went along that Adriana had it together on the day of the exam, that she'd aced it, because I sensed it was what my mother would have preferred. When I came home from college years later, while we sat in the same living room, she on that same couch, I told her I was seriously considering becoming a schoolteacher myself. She didn't react as though I was selling myself short, the way many I mentioned the idea of my working as a kindergarten teacher to did. She looked pleased and surprised at the possibility that I might end up morphing into just as much of my mother's daughter as my father's.

ALS (Lou Gehrig's disease) killed her when I was 25 years old, the same year I moved to New York. She died before I could ask why she, generally a shy woman, chose a career that involved daily public speaking; before I thought to ask why she chose French and to work with teenagers; before I could ask what she did for lunch during her workdays, since I never saw her pack or carry one for herself and she wasn't the type to splurge on already-made soups and sandwiches; before we had a chance to take on Paris together.

***

Paris is not the best place for dining out when you're trying to drop a couple of dress sizes. The bread, cheese, pastries, rich butter- and cream-based entrées. Even so, I guess it's true about French women not getting fat. Not the ones out and about that week. Their epic meals might have something to do with it. Savoring saves you? I had a *café crème* and a *pain au chocolat* at a supposed quickie café on the stimulating Boulevard Saint-Germain. The diners at the end of my seating area, and the diners behind them, were stimulated by one another and their meals so much I remained trapped in a corner after wolfing down mine. There was no discreet way to get past the chairs of those seated on my side of the situation. If I were half the woman I'd been a week earlier, I would have dropped to my hands and knees and crawled to freedom under the table. Instead, I quietly studied my Fodor's guidebook, reading engaging write-ups of museums, shops, and landmarks located in close walking distance of this very café, at my fingertips, out of my reach. (Prior to that week, I took ordering a coffee to go, and roaming around with it, completely for granted.)

During a walk along the Left Bank of the Seine, I crossed paths with another probable slow eater who bent down to pick up someone's well-worn wedding band from the sidewalk.

"Do you think it's real gold?" she asked in English, with a thick French accent. Locals intuitively realized I wasn't one of theirs.

"*Possible*," I said, in my best French drawl, as she tried it on. My mom often corrected my French pronunciations, as did most other French speakers. I can do voices, not accents.

"It's too big for me," she said. "But you should take it. It could fit *you*."

Was she *une comédienne?* That ring was almost the size of some bracelets I've seen.

"No thanks."

"No, really, why not? Take it. A souvenir from Paris."

Yes, that's just the souvenir I was holding out for. A marriage memento a critically obese man has lost and is probably frantically searching for. The day before, I fell on a sheet of ice. That memory is a more precious souvenir than the wedding ring could ever have been. I take tumbles all the time, but never down the street from the legendary Moulin Rouge! When I stood up to soldier on, the red windmill spun without stopping overhead, waving goodbye.

***

I saw it all that week. Notre-Dame, the Panthéon, Napoleon's tomb, the Tuileries and Luxembourg Gardens. I futzed around Victor Hugo's old digs and made myself at home in the Phantom of the Opera's house, instantly understanding why he didn't want to leave. I spent half a day at the Palace of Versailles and explored every nook and cranny of the Shakespeare & Co. bookstore Gertrude Stein and James Joyce frequented. You name it, I probably toured it. By the end of each night, my feet were in so much pain I worried about not being able to use them the following morning. Coming home dog-tired suggests the day or night wasn't wasted, or so I told myself during my spring-chicken days.

In Père Lachaise Cemetery, I spent more than an hour trying to find Édith Piaf's gravesite. At the time, I didn't know much about her other than that we both used to sing and have dealt with despair. I'd expected something larger, surrounded by more open space. Maybe some birds chirping atop or fluttering around it, even in 40-degree weather. Earlier in the hour, a golf cart filled with groundskeepers led me to another singer's, Jim Morrison's, small gravesite, unremarkably draped with flowers and a photo of him.

"*C'est tout?*" I asked before they drove off.

"*C'est tout*," they answered, not that impressed with my not being that impressed.

There was a tree next to Morrison's plot with messages and lettering carved into and written on its trunk, cigarette butts stuck to it with already-been-chewed gum as glue. It's my most fervent memory of my trip to any cemetery, places where I more commonly feel, if anything, inappropriately distracted. I want a forest of trees like that around my own gravesite. Go easy with the roses, heavy with the written words, saying what you mean in permanent print, as long as it's genuinely sweet or funny.

I tried getting the Pigalle metro station agent to reimburse me for the extra, expired 24-hour subway card I was erroneously sold, after it turned out that a station agent from the day before and I had had a minimum of two different conversations. This second agent couldn't understand what I asked for either but owned it. He handed me his desktop computer's keyboard to type what I said in

English, and it straight away translated into French on his screen. He typed his answer in French and the computer translated it into English for me.

No, was the gist of his response. Reimbursement was not an option.

This may have been the moment and the metro station that first made me think of my mom's last time in town. Did she get around on the Métro? She must have, but I never heard her mention being in a subway car and I can't picture her underground.

I fell again, while crossing a street. Time for more wine!

"*Une personne*," I said to the nearest bistro's bartender. He roughly gestured for me to take a seat somewhere, anywhere, out of his direct line of vision. I expected him to bring me a menu. He brought me a Stella draft and a bill for 3.50 euros, and never returned. I drank up and flipped through the Fodor's book, which I'd all but memorized.

We reunited at the bar, where I paid my tab. "*Quelle direction est le Louvre?*" I asked, while he counted out my change. Forget about my sorry accent or that I can barely understand any spoken French prattled off in my presence. I could *read* nearly all of the written French I came across, so the "proficient in French" bit at the bottom of my résumé can hang tight. At least that's what I thought and continue to think, although this bartender probably wouldn't agree. He lost his mind, just couldn't hold onto it. Something about his refusal to speak in English, even though he may have spoken English better than I do. The thunderous mini-meltdown was so flamboyant I started laughing. His boys around the bar looked at and then away from him with mounting disbelief, as they, too, had a hard time processing what we were in the middle of. When even your drunk-ass, countrymen cronies are too embarrassed to support you—that's when you know it's Last Call. Simmer down at a back-room table and sip a lukewarm Stella of your own.

Family, friends, Hemingway, the media—each influence led me to believe that Paris would change me. It has. I had never been so overjoyed to be an American, had never missed New York City so much, and hadn't felt so lost or lonely in ages. Self-sufficiency gets talked up as something admirable, a gift, a sign of competence and inner strength. There's also such a thing as too much self-sufficiency, a fine line between hyper-independence and isolation. I hadn't expected isolation during this trip, thinking I'd at least find an amazing make-out buddy, a French kiss. It was Valentine's Day week *in Paris*. If this wasn't the time and place for love or lust to bombard every particle of the atmosphere, when and where was? As worn out and depressed as I was, I should have danced in the streets with the fishmonger who asked me to meet up with him for drinks after I asked for directions back to the guest house at the end of another punishing day of tourism. He wasn't too proud to speak English. We could have married by now. He could have eased my access to fresh flounder. I could have smuggled him out of France.

In the years since my mom died, I've connected more naturally with older women than with most people who are my age. The mothers of new acquaintances instead of the acquaintances themselves. The 65-year-old co-workers instead of those in their twenties and thirties. Too many people my age have come to feel younger than me, we don't exactly get each other, the divide can grow uncomfortable.

Although we didn't talk much about her last trip there, I remember my mom mentioning that she sat on a bench by the Eiffel Tower for a long rest break. I more clearly recall pouting about not having been included in her trip. Lots of mothers and daughters took those kinds of duo trips together. I knew it then and know it even more now. From time to time, mothers and daughters visiting New York stop me to get directions or ask me to snap a picture of them on their rental bikes. Good for them, a little devastating for me. There are times when I miss my mom so much that even the air I breathe comes off as oppressive. Nobody has consistently made the effort to try to understand me, nobody has forgiven me, nobody has made me look more closely at myself and my future the way my mother did. In one of her final days, she said she'd stay with me in spirit, and it took years to figure out what this meant, how that worked. I rarely visit her grave. I've only felt her presence elsewhere, anywhere. I can now often tell when she's around.

Sometimes it's anticlimactic to take in the great wonders of the world you've only seen photos and video footage of up close, but the Eiffel Tower managed to blow my mind in person. After circling it a couple of times, I stood directly underneath it, holding back my head and staring straight up into its belly, all the way to the top. I've wanted to do that since middle school, maybe before then. I cared nothing about riding the elevator to see an aerial view of the city from the tower's highest point, or fine dining at one of the restaurants on the first and second levels. For me, it was only ever about standing directly underneath and looking through it toward the sky.

Afterwards, I sat on a nearby bench for a while. A small, yappy white dog appeared, searching for his ball. He let me pet him, making it clear he didn't need or particularly enjoy my touch; it was a one-time shot, an act of charity. I usually prefer dogs to their owners, but an exception suddenly sat down next to me. She was energetic, in her fifties or sixties, unpretentiously dressed, all brightness, broad smiles, pointed eye contact. We took turns throwing the dog's dirty ball out into the distance and breaking into soft, easy laughter at the sight of his maniacal hustling for it. We chatted about what I'd seen and done in town, what I still hoped to accomplish. Radiating childlike excitement about everything I said, everything she said, everything the dog did, she gently corrected my French pronunciations. By the time she stood up, warmly smiling at me one last time, and slowly headed back in the direction she and her fluffy child had come from, Paris had faded into someplace less foreign.

***

Let's celebrate one more piece of practical wisdom my mom slipped into my head—if you don't like something about your life, you can usually change it. It's all about determination and mindset modification. I chose to stop treating the rest of that week like a bad audition, something to power through. No more moping along the boulevards where Vespas zoom at you out of nowhere and pedestrians bring little baguettes to their lips, the way I longed to do with a large and sturdy paper cup of black coffee. I finally got myself to Paris, dammit. That week, I stood inches away from renowned Degas and Renoir paintings I'd only admired as cheap poster replicas or in the huge art books my mom colorfully wrapped up for me at Christmas. I climbed the staircases of graffitied subway stations more mesmerizing than the works hanging in the Musée d'Orsay. I ate *madeleines* and *macarons* that weren't stale.

On my last day in Sophisticationville, I window-shopped my way through the fashionable Marais district, *ooh la la*, hunting for a unique Parisian knick-knack to have and to hold, to love and to cherish, 'til death did me in. Death and dying can ambush you at any time, no matter how hale and hearty you think you are. You could get run down by a Vespa on the far-off Champs-Élysées or on the avenue on which you've lived for a lifetime. You could drink or drug your way to the end. You could get blindsided by an unpreventable, uncompromising disease that will give the whole concept of mindset overhaul a run for its money.

The last time my mom was on or around the Champs-Élysées, she brought me back a heavy black bottle of Chanel No. 5. I may have idly sprayed it into the air a couple of times but have never worn it. For years, it sat on the dresser of my childhood bedroom like a trophy, beneath a gigantic Senior Music Award plaque from high school. Not well-versed in designer labels, even my younger self knew Chanel was big time, much higher end than my drugstore bottles of Tabu or Malibu Musk. As my mom is the one who taught me not to settle for less than high quality, but to avoid paying full price for it, her voice is often in my head when I shop for business suits and formalwear, cookware and appliances, luggage and jewelry. I bought a pair of good gold earrings two years after Paris because they are timeless and go with everything. The first night I took them off and put them away I realized they're something she would have invested in, stud versions of the tiny hoops that perennially hung from her earlobes. Although I wasn't vocal about it until the summer night she followed me out onto our back stoop to confirm her months were numbered, I viewed my mom the way she viewed Paris.

"Lose yourself in this neighborhood," Fodor's said. I sure did, walking around the Marais in circles for at least an hour trying to find a famed falafel stand. My peripheral vision is sick; I'm staggeringly aware of my surroundings, even when it seems like I'm open-eyed meditating. I noticed a wiry older man notice my handbag. He stood at the side of the street I strode down, finishing off the last of his cigarette, looking back and forth from the body of my bag to its thick straps, the wheels in his small, pointy head turning like the spokes of the Moulin Rouge windmill. I grabbed the straps with tough love, pulling the bag closer to me, and picked up the pace. A brand-new necklace and polka-dot toiletries bag were in there, and I would do whatever it took to protect them. He saw and understood my quick-thinking maneuvers, resented them, and glared at me in a way I'd been glared at only four or five other times in my life, three of those times having been in other parts of this city, earlier in the week.

A few minutes into what I assumed had been my escape, I sensed a wicked, unsettling presence, not far from me, much closer than before. I swiveled my head around, and there he was, two feet behind me, not taking his eyes off mine, sneering up a storm. The third degree that followed was slow, menacing, low-volumed:

"*Vous avez….?*" "*Vous avez….?*" "*Mais oui….?*" Blah, blah, blah.

I don't know all of what he was saying, just that every other word of it was terrible. An interpreter would have helped, as would that French-to-English translating program from the metro station. If my smartphone had been bright enough to pull it up in this time zone, the vitriol could have been all spelled out for me. The story would be livelier, more complete:

> *"You have something you want to hide from me?*
>
> *You have something you don't want me to take? Is that right?*
>
> *You'd like if I put a freshly lit cigarette out on one of your cheeks before pushing you down onto this chic cobblestone corner?"*

Only one of us had the foresight to wear running shoes.

BALLAD OF THE BALLOT

Ten or so days into my first semester of college, I came down with the urge to run for office, although I forget what my title would have been. A freshman representative? An East Campus envoy? Who knew? My last-minute campaigning consisted of walking door to door, floor to floor, through my dorm with a girl who lived down the hall from me one weekday afternoon, collecting enough signatures to get my name on the ballot. It was one of the weirdest whims I'd had in at least a month (I don't know if I ended up voting for myself, or voting at all, when Judgment Day came, and am not positive about whether I so much as properly submitted that signature sheet), but not a bad way to meet our new neighbors who came from all over the country and were trying to figure out what we were supposed to be figuring out. After my quiet defeat at the polls, I tried out for an a cappella group, losing that bid too, and my fascination with both politics and music has only skyrocketed since.

I turned 18 that October of 1996, during a bigger, more talked-about election season. A presidential one, the

70

kind of president with an office in the White House instead of a student union building. Coming from Ohio (a swing state) but going to school in North Carolina (then a red state), that fall I planned on swinging for Bill Clinton (the darling of blue states and blue families like mine) by way of a mailed-in absentee ballot.[6] I'd looked forward to becoming old enough to vote for years, even more than I looked forward to going away to college. We all have certain aspects of legal adulthood that provide a major sense of relief about no longer being 16 years old. For some, it might be the freedom of sitting in someone's basement with a case of Bud Light or a magnum-sized bottle of sauvignon blanc without having to hide a drop. For others, it could be eating a magnum-sized bag of popcorn for dinner and staying up all night to finish a book without flashlights or arguments. Then there's the minimized hormonal stuff. And not having to walk past your school gym in between classes only to see it full of voting booths you can't meaningfully enter because 16-year-olds can't vote for anything outside of school elections.

Election Day has become my Super Bowl Sunday or Oscars night (I don't love watching football or movies). In my twenties, aside from a 2004 primary race when I unexpectedly found myself back home in Ohio for many

---

[6] According to official records, I first voted in March 1996...but didn't vote in the November 1996 election. I have no memory of what went wrong with obtaining or mailing in my general election absentee ballot that year, but suspect I have no one but myself to blame.

months, I voted through the US mail, paranoid about my precious ballot getting lost or marginalized. A mailbox is more impersonal and carries less gravitas and grandeur than a privacy booth—that idea gnawed on me more by the year, well before the US got slammed by the coronavirus pandemic in 2020, and mailed-in ballots became the safest course of civic action for many people, at least for the time being.[7] Pre-corona, I persuaded myself that we need to go live to thrive.

So, in 2011, I registered as a New York State voter, seven years after moving to New York City, because my Ohio registration lapsed (more on that soon) and I wanted to vote in local elections that had some direct impact on my could-always-be-better local life. I was hyped to vote in person in the next available election, a minor primary I learned of from a mailed notice from New York's board of elections. Having no idea who was running, I planned to vote for people with ethnic names, and if the candidates expected anything better, they should have campaigned harder instead of acting like me in college. I hadn't received a single flyer from anyone running, no "I *will* fight for the Average Joe" promises or "my opponent is trash, and here's a sampling of reasons why" condemnations or pictures of anyone sitting on some front steps with an unrealistically

---

[7] Although, since my absentee ballot for the June 2020 New York primary arrived in the mail the day before the election, I ended up marching into my polling location on Election Day, in a camouflage mask (my I Mean Business mask), to drop off the sealed envelope in person.

wholesome-looking family of five. That Tuesday night, I strode into my empty polling station, ready to get to work, forgetting what booth voting entailed, wondering if there'd be refreshments. But there was no line and no privacy booths were set up because there was no longer an election in my district that day. Two surly security guards shooed me away.

***

The 2008 US presidential election was no ho-hum affair. It was the first time a non-white person had won a party nomination, and a pretty extraordinary non-white person to boot. During the buildup to Election Day, I rode a bus to the Wilkes-Barre, Pennsylvania, area to canvass (something I had never done for a candidate before and have never ended up doing for one since) for Barack Obama, going door to door in a white working-class neighborhood, where almost every household enthusiastically had his back. That summer and fall, there was so much energy and anticipation, so much to lose if another Republican succeeded two terms of George W. Bush and twenty-first-century Americans proclaimed they wouldn't permit certain patterns and traditions to change.

That fall, I innocently waited for my absentee ballot (or at least something in reference to it) to arrive in the mail. And waited. *Shouldn't it have come by now?* I thought at some point before the big day. I asked my dad if anything came to his/our house and he said no. I think he might have been the one who called the board of elections and was told my Ohio voter registration had lapsed and the deadline to renew in time for the upcoming election had passed. By that time, New York's voter registration deadline had passed as well. Here was the most important presidential election of my generation, thus far, one I'd crossed state lines to campaign for, and I wasn't allowed to weigh in for reasons I remain uncomfortable with.

I googled "why can't convicted felons vote?" (I had grown to develop a kinship with the felons in the midst of my additional confusion about why so many who finish their prison and other sentencing terms get barred from voting, like I did.) Some believe that those with felony convictions shouldn't vote because they have broken "the social contract." That's it? How many times did I break that thing in the months leading up to November 2008? Plenty of US citizens have behaved worse than I have, and they still have a say in who becomes the next comptroller. Contracts are like people—they can expire or be amended. What's the point of releasing people from prison only to have them sit idly by (while still having to file taxes and worry about passing background checks) as all those around them elect someone whose stances affect countless aspects of the rest of their lives?

In the years since then, I've thought about this debacle from time to time. I remember keeping up with my Ohio absentee voting in the major elections prior to November 2008, but (if that had been the case) why didn't I get what should have come to me? I must have dropped the ball somewhere. In 2020 (you read that right), I called the Cuyahoga County Board of Elections, asking if I could go over my Ohio voting history with them. The nice midwestern boy I got on the phone (who said my name came up in their system as "canceled") ran down my record, in reverse chronological order.

"Let's see, as far as absentee voting, you voted in March 2008, November 2006, November 2004, Novem—"

"Did you say March *2008?*"

"Yup."

I know not to lose my shit on customer service representatives or their equivalents. It's been ingrained in me, from a very young age, that they usually have nothing to do with the infuriating verdicts they deliver.

Maybe there was a miscommunication (but on whose part)? Or something got lost in the mail? Why didn't I ask about what was going on with my absentee ballot earlier than I did?[8] And a country that can invent crash test dummies and the swivel chair can't find a way to turn same-day registration into a nationwide nicety?

Ten years after 2008 (with the backdrop of a professional pussy-grabber ruling all the land), the US Supreme Court gave a major green light to what I now refer to as the state of Ohio's let's-purge-the-voter-rolls game (these are not the midwestern values I know or stand behind). This

---

[8] THIS IS WHERE I DROPPED THE BALL.

federal case came by way of an Ohio man who learned his registration had lapsed when he arrived at his polling station in 2015.[9] Unlike me, he hadn't voted in a while. He also, like me (and like my dad, back at my Ohio mailing address), didn't recall an update-your-address notice having come in the mail (although I don't know why I would have been sent one of those if I'd voted as recently as eight months before the election I got kicked out of). Being at the receiving end of a purge when you're least expecting it is the absolute worst. A 2019 *New York Times* article, about how "strict" the state of Ohio's voting laws have been, reported that the head of the Ohio League of Women Voters had her name flagged as an inactive voter (meaning they were about to drop her from the rolls)—even though she voted three times in the previous year.[10]

***

One night during that 2008 election cycle, while I still assumed I'd be voting that fall, I went to dinner with people who said they won't vote in presidential general elections on principle. They laughed that exercise off, with the specific excuse seeming to revolve around the 2000 presidential election fiasco and the Electoral College, this Electoral College they deemed far mightier than either of them.

---

[9] *Husted v. A. Philip Randolph Institute*, 584 US __(2018).
[10] Nicholas Casey, "Ohio Was Set to Purge 235,000 Voters. It Was Wrong About 20%," *New York Times*, October 14, 2019.

"But the Electoral College has only really come into play when the popular vote was neck and neck. If Al Gore's popular vote lead had been something closer to 70 percent in the 2000 election wouldn't he have won, and the Electoral College not have mattered as much?" I asked.

"Well, yeah," they admitted. "Nobody ever talks to us like this," one added, as if they ran with the Crips or the Gambinos instead of with self-righteous socialists who flocked to every local protest and rally they could find, sometimes making it clear they judged little ole me for not filling my own free time with protests and rallies, but couldn't be bothered to occasionally stand in a voting line the way they stood in line at coffee shops, bars, or restaurants every week. They wanted to occupy Wall Street, yet could barely fathom the idea of occupying a polling booth to help elect people who would have more authority to clip Wall Street's (and many others') wings than they do.

When it comes to big-picture causes, like the rights and welfare of the non-wealthy or non-white men, I can't afford to donate huge amounts of money. If I publish a blog post or think piece that advocates on behalf of a big-picture cause, or attend a protest or rally, how do I know how many minds I've actually swayed, that I'm not just preaching to or marching with the choir? None of these acts are wastes of time, but when I'm given the choice between two or more candidates, going on record to check off boxes to declare the ones I want feels like something more tangible, giving me more peace of mind that I became a formal part of a historically consequential decision.

***

By the time the 2012 presidential election rolled around, I finally got to cast my vote for Obama, less than two weeks after an unsuccessful attempt to board an overbooked bus to Pennsylvania to canvass for him again, ready for another round of the first US president whose name ends in a vowel (I mean a real vowel—not a technicality vowel like Monroe, Pierce, or Coolidge), and didn't mind standing outside for an hour in the cold to secure that tangibility. Voting is the easiest way to convince myself I'm contributing something useful to the society outside of my household, social circle, and workplace. Most Election Days are tinted with hope, more people carry themselves with purpose, they've got a post-coital glow, even during an election cycle that left a huge swath of Americans demoralized, like in 2016. Unless the lines are long enough to make you late for something or there's been a surprise disenfranchisement incident at the check-in table, people walking into or out of a polling location rarely look mad or sad, just watch the next time you're at or passing by one.[11] Registered voters who may have been feeling like failures in other areas of their lives now have this notch in their belts. They did something significant and targeted and productive, at least

---

[11] I'm talking about Election Day proper here. I found the vibe (and length) of the only early voting line I ever almost joined indistinguishable from that of a peak-hour procession in (or outside of) a Manhattan Trader Joe's.

on that particular day of that given year. Casting a vote involves an outcome I can concretely help control, and I seek out as many of those moments as possible to help maintain my composure in a world too dominated by destiny.

After in-person voting in the 2012 US presidential general election, I got on the subway and went to work.

After in-person voting in the 2016 US presidential general election, I went straight from my polling site to the nearest church, followed by a walk along the Hudson River, to try taking the edges off. Donald Trump officially became the winner later that night, again because of the Electoral College, since so many either didn't care enough to vote or were prevented from doing so. I was one of those who took this news hard. Not as melodramatically as some of the kids I saw in the press footage, mind you, in that I never threw my hand to my mouth and wept, fishing for a hug from a similarly affected neighbor whose theatrics had mine beat. I do, however, recall taking a very deep breath and rubbing my eyes with my fingers, before pensively looking off into the distance, asking myself whether this could be a sign of the end of the world—week after week, for months. I told one of the most politically apathetic Ohioans I know (who voted for Hillary Clinton, after almost not voting at all) that she'll always be able to say that she went out and did something to keep this from happening. When I seriously considered moving back to Middle America, Ohio's swing state stature was as much of an allure as the lower cost of living.

After in-person voting in the 2020 US presidential general election, I went grocery shopping. What's more interesting is how on the Halloween night (a few days earlier) preceding it, I gazed up at the blue moon shining above my neighborhood and openly prayed to the universe, "Please don't let the pussy-grabber win, please don't let the pussy-grabber win, please don't let the pussy-grabber win." And, you're welcome, it worked.

***

Years before Donald Trump finally lost, on the night of the 2013 New York City mayoral race, I stopped into my local Rite Aid for marked-down Halloween candy, earbuds firmly in place. An older man walking toward me asked what I was listening to and I told him it was Tracy Chapman's "All That You Have Is Your Soul."

"The girl with the tied-up hair?" he asked.

He wondered if he could have a listen. I took out a bud and held it to his ear, right when she (yet another Cleveland, Ohio, native) sung the chorus, and I couldn't have asked for a better tune or message to have entered our time and space.

"That's her," he said, smiling.

Although he said he didn't vote because he knew the candidate he wanted to win (Bill de Blasio) would go on to win, even he gave off the Election Day glow. Even he recognized the power of the day, the chance to make revisions, the opportunity for another shot, like getting another freshman year all over again.

SHIFTING GEARS

In a woman's world, three and five—when thrown together, in that order, without a space in between—are red-letter numbers. I'd heard and read about 35 since before turning 25, and largely blame the steady rise of the 24-hour "news" cycles, which made it clear that men must only deal with two milestone birthdays between the ages of 30 and 40—their 30th and 40th. Whereas women reach an additional milestone at the halfway mark, the only half-marathon some of us can hope to qualify for. They say 35 is the age at which our eggs start to rot for real.

For those of us without children, but who still want them, 35 is when the biological clock (which once tick-tocked away, the way a reliable but soundless wristwatch might) has developed into more of an obnoxiously beeping alarm clock you can figure out how to turn down but can't completely shut off. Thirty-five is when many modern-day, child-free American women decide they want to break free from this freedom and seriously start stressing about family planning.

Whereas, for me, 35 was when I seriously started thinking about getting my driver's license.

My mom had me in her late thirties and my brother in her early forties, so I figured my genes were pretty decent in that department. Also, there was always adoption, and I still had many years to realistically try that. So first things first, instead of batting my eyelashes through singles' mixers or jumping onto online dating sites, I threw myself into an hour's worth of Google searching, price-shopping uptown driving schools, the cheaper and closer to where I lived, the better. About 15 months later, I signed up with one of them. Less than seven months after that, I drove my friend Rhonda from New York to Cleveland and back, a drive that ended up lasting close to 12 hours each way. I come from Cleveland, two of her siblings lived in Cleveland, and neither of us had more interesting Fourth of July weekend plans or were that fazed by the idea of two under-experienced license holders driving a total of 1,000 miles in holiday weekend traffic on I-80.

***

Moments after walking through the revolving doors of the rental car agency at LaGuardia Airport, Rhonda announced that she no longer held a valid driver's license. Something about losing her purse at a football game earlier that year and never following up after the license expired. The tentative plan had always been that I'd do all the driving on this maiden voyage (my first road trip as a driver, my first time driving an SUV), and she'd mainly ride along as back-up and moral support—this new information ensured that's exactly what we could expect.

When the front desk agent asked to see my license, I pulled it out and passed it over as if it were a PhD or an action shot of me with Diana Ross, so pleased with myself was I. Up until getting a New York State ID card many years earlier, I handed bouncers, bartenders, and TSA agents my beat-up but barely used passport. By that Friday morning, this license had sat in my wallet for close to two months. I learned how to drive in Upper Manhattan that past winter, mostly during rush hour and other high-stakes conditions. "Wow!" my dad wrote back when I emailed him after finishing my first lesson. Even he refuses to drive in New York City. One of the toughest and most naturally confident people I know—not to mention the greatest driver within my phone's contacts list—is scared to drive in New York, and I had just done it for close to an hour, so I was onto something big. By the time I'd left home for college, it seems as though nobody in my family ever expected me to become a driver, legally or otherwise. "What is the year of that car you came in?" my dad asked, addressing me by my brother's name, the day after I'd driven home from New York, before realizing he had the wrong kid. "I never thought I'd be asking you that question," he admitted, laughing. "I don't associate you with driving."

It's not unusual to be in your mid-thirties and single in New York City. It's also not unusual to be in your mid-thirties and not able to drive in New York City. What *is* unusual is someone who lives in New York City but didn't grow up in New York City not knowing how to drive. That was my demographic and I think most of us who fall into it wound up in big, public transportation-heavy urban centers for reasons we don't often realize, much less talk about. The idea of me behind the wheel has rarely seemed harmless. I can think of only one time, as a teenager, when I had any burning desire to slide into a driver's seat and go. My friend Kristen and I were sitting outside my house, dead bored. To liven things up, I snuck my mom's keys out of her purse, after waiting for the right moment, so we could cruise around the neighborhood, in broad daylight, neither of us old enough to apply for a learner's permit. My inspiration had come earlier that summer, when three girls in my grade ran-skipped to my front porch to tell me and Kristen how they'd just driven someone's parents' car around the block, well underage. "We drove the car, we drove the car!" all three cried out, jumping up and down with enough excitement to make me want to experience a rush like that too. *Look at the sorts of things my contemporaries are doing, how they're spending their summer break, instead of lounging on a porch all day.*

We never made it out of the garage. Kristen was smart enough to refuse to climb in next to me. "Buckle up," she yelled after I revved the engine. I was smart enough not to go through with it, in part because I didn't know how or where to change the gears. I didn't know what a "gear" was. In the years leading up to 16, I hadn't thought to watch

85

where my parents' and other chauffeurs' hands specifically went when they backed up, or went from backing up to moving forward. That's how low my interest was in learning how to master this skill.

***

I got my first learner's permit at age 16 or 17 on the west side of Cleveland. After completing my required eight hours of driving around town with an instructor, I continued practicing with my parents, who both had years of teaching experience. Teaching in classrooms. Teaching academic subjects. Teaching people who were not related to them. They are the reason my jitters and indifference about learning how to drive blew up into a larger-than-life chronic fear. Their "YOU DON'T KNOW WHAT YOU'RE DOING, YOU'LL GET US ALL KILLED!" approach didn't work for me. The screaming, the dramatic sighing and jumpy reflexes, the half-incredulous/half-nasty faces they made, distracting me out of the corner of my eye.

Riding shotgun, my dad used to let me drive his car to my weekly candy-striping shift at a local hospital. On one of those drives, I made a left-hand turn at a semi-busy intersection. "That was a good turn," he said, and I've always remembered that moment (whenever I've been back at that intersection, I vividly replay in my head how good those five words felt) because it was the only driving-related compliment he'd ever given me. My mom, on the other hand, never complimented anything she watched me do

LIVING OF NATURAL CAUSES

behind the wheel. When I told them my driver's ed teacher implied I was well on my way to becoming a great driver, they implied this meant something was wrong with him, too.

One sunny afternoon, I tried backing out from the curvier bottom of the driveway instead of from the middle, where my parents usually parked the car for me before my drives. Since I'd had very little experience maneuvering in reverse, I wasn't good at it, as my mom made sure to point out, rather than step-by-step telling me what to do with the wheel in order to back out along the narrow curve more proficiently. She criticized and yelled, I yelled back, fed up and flustered, more aggravated than I had been during all these weeks of counter-productive family lessons, which was what led me to mistake the accelerator for the brake. Or what led me to *slam* on the accelerator instead of slamming on the brake. I lost control of the car and crashed into the garage. As soon as the car came to a complete stop, I silently stormed out of it and into my bedroom, swearing off driving from that day forward. I feared driving a car the way wealthy Los Angeles residents feared the Manson family in and/or after the summer of '69.

***

In my mid-thirties, I was a different kind of gal. More of a broad than a gal, which made the world, and my place in it, seem less overwhelming. There are different degrees of fears and different importance levels involved with conquering them. For example, I also have a fear of bungee jumping. But unlike flying off a platform with a cord attached to you for no reason beyond an adrenaline rush, knowing how to drive a car is a valuable, life-enhancing, potentially life-saving skill. As more weeks and months of adulthood passed by, I decided I had to know what to do in the event I ever needed to drive a drunkard home from an out-of-town house party, or my future child to the hospital, or a getaway car. During road trips, my childlike inability to contribute to the driving truly began to trouble me. Several job postings I came across had "valid driver's license" as an application requirement; not for any job I had my heart set on, but I've never loved the idea of unnecessarily limiting my options. On top of all this, my widowed father was in his seventies—spry and healthy, but in his seventies. As if worrying about my own future wasn't bad enough, I worried about his, knowing that when he eventually came to really need my help, I wouldn't be of much use to him in suburban Middle America without a driver's license. The passivity of passengering, the having to do it, became too much. I had gradually gained notoriety as someone who dexterously sat in the driver's seat of her own life—except when it came to four-wheel vehicles with a muffler and built-in climate control system.

The morning I showed up at the Upper Manhattan driving school for road lesson #1, the guy who owned the place told me Gabriela was waiting for me outside. "Who's Gabriela?" I asked.

Gabriela was my driving teacher who sat in a double-parked, student-driver car a little farther up on Broadway. After we quickly introduced ourselves, she told me to get behind the wheel and take off. "Aren't we going to practice in a parking lot or something first?" I asked. "No parking lots, *mami*," she said, "We drive the streets." I briefly explained my driving history to her and she didn't care, helping me believe that my driving past had nothing to do with the driving I was capable of doing, moving forward. And with that, I got off to a singularly successful start, not screwing anything up until 15 minutes into it. Whenever I did screw up (like when I could have run over a pedestrian in a crosswalk, or careened into a bus, or mowed down a parked car), she hit the brake on her side of the car while expertly grabbing the right side of the steering wheel. "Easy, *mami*, easy on the gas."

While nervously waiting to get picked up for lesson #3, I thought about quitting, postponing this latest adventurous crap I'd taken up for a later date, maybe saving it for when I turned 40. I wondered whether my pre-paid 10-lesson package was refundable because I lived in New York, where I didn't need to drive to get around. What was I trying to prove, and why? When the student-driver car pulled up in front of my building, I saw we had a special guest— a middle-aged woman who had just finished her fifth lesson, and now I had to drop her off somewhere else. "I'm addicted to driving," she said from the backseat, as I buckled up, checked my mirrors, and fruitlessly tried pushing back my seat. "Are you?" I asked. "I crashed my dad's car in our driveway when I was a teenager and, until a few weeks ago, never drove again," I shared as I looked behind me before pulling out and driving up my busy street. Three blocks later, we almost got into a major collision when I was about to make a left turn. Afterwards, even Gabriela the Great stayed noticeably rattled for several minutes, as she silently noshed on a strand of beef jerky.

I'm more addicted to being driven. Long car rides, taking the scenic routes and longest way home. I've loved riding in cars, especially in the backseat, where it's the easiest to sprawl out and think. There's too much pressure to talk and be "on" when you're sitting up front. And, just physically, getting into the driver's seat, with that huge wheel sticking out and in the way, is annoying. I mean, come on, you can't even put your feet up or anything.

***

Always so much traffic getting into or out of Manhattan. Everyone wants to come to or bust out of this borough. Now add the first day of holiday weekend traffic to this. To my immediate right, I had the most venerated prom queen of the Eastern Seaboard. Nearly everyone who meets Rhonda becomes magnetically drawn to her. She's bubbly and sparkly, the most popular girl in the world. My polar opposite in close to every way—lavishly extroverted, she's fond of things like people, crowds, trends, relentless sunshine. On this drive to Cleveland and back, her phone wouldn't stop popping off. The calls, the texts, the emails streaming into different apps and accounts she managed, a different sound effect for each form of communication, including one that sounded like a honking horn, convincing me I was taking up two lanes and we were about to crash, until I made her switch off all the racket. (On the other side of the car, my phone vibrated no more than a few times, round trip. One text might have been a wrong number.)

Rhonda didn't pass her road test on the first try. Her referee failed her before the test really began for over-hesitating before pulling out of a Washington, DC, parking lot. This taught me that not even extreme charm could secure a win and, in the weeks leading up to it, passing my own road test became my most pressing psychological preoccupation.

Once an honors student, always an honors student—the idea of failing a test was terrifying. I'd aced the written exam, but knew the actual, manual driving part would be my true hurdle. I found comfort in the living reality that almost every moronic, inept wack job I've dealt with has had a driver's license. So what if some may have had theirs suspended? If *they* managed to land the license in the first place, how hard could this be? "Most of this stuff is just common sense," Gabriela said during one of my early lessons, without understanding this meant nothing to me yet, that not everyone's idea of logic is experienced equally. I mastered some of the "common sense" work involved with driving the way I used to get As in math classes—by memorizing and then applying formulas. Parallel parking = turn the wheel one rotation to the right and back up until the passenger-side mirror lines up with the license plate of the car you're parking behind; turn the wheel as far as it will go to the left and keep reversing until you're good and in; turn the wheel two rotations to the right before putting the car in park. Gabriela patiently taught me how to drive by the book, and I passed my road test on the first try (although not with flying colors), and got my license at age 36, 20 years behind schedule.

***

I wanted to become an excellent driver instead of just a competent one. I wanted everyone getting into a car with me to later tell others, "damn that girl can drive," the way I characterize my dad and my dad has characterized two of my uncles. Regular practice was the only way to get there, which wasn't easy for someone in a pedestrian-, public transportation-, and taxi-oriented town. Within 48 hours of receiving my hard-copy license, I opened a Zipcar ("the world's largest car-sharing and car-club service") membership. Within 48 hours of receiving my Zipcard, I reserved a car, and less than 24 hours after making that reservation, I was back on the road, this time as a licensed driver, nobody at my side. I used the Zipcar to joyride in and around the city close to once a week for about five weeks, before the Cleveland trip. Uptown, downtown, crosstown through the park, all around the East River Plaza parking garage, speeding along the West Side Highway and Saw Mill River Parkway.

Even as a licensed driver, no matter how many times I get behind the wheel, I'm scared about operating this dangerous, potentially deadly machine. I no longer avoid something just out of fear. But before I jump into doing something I fear, I tend to incessantly bitch about how on edge I am to anyone who's lucky enough to be around at the time, detailing all that could go wrong. As I walk up to a car I'm about to set in motion, I'll have somehow convinced myself I have forgotten how to make clean turns or that I'll hit a cocky recreational cyclist who suddenly glides in front of my bumper. I think I'll crash and burn. Once my foot hits the pedal and my hands spring into action, it all comes back to me without any deep thought, like going for a bike ride—even in the craziest city in America with its uniquely aggressive pedestrian culture, as well as the bikers, skateboarders, and motorized wheelchairs zooming alongside and weaving in between moving cars. It's fight or flight, and I throw down until the whistle blows. As soon as I shift the gear back into park, when it's all over and everything has gone fine, I smile and strut for the rest of the day as if I've just woken up, cheerfully confused, from a dream.[12]

---

[12] I most likely wrote an early draft of the paragraph you just read before getting into a Zipcar fender bender, on the morning of my birthday, while backing up and pulling out of a tight parking space,

The rental car to Cleveland was my first time, as an adult, driving a car with no signage on it, my first time driving without advertising something—no student-driver placard on the roof, or Zipcar logo and pricing info emblazoned on the doors. Although we've been BFFs since college and now lived within a 90-minute subway ride of each other, Rhonda and I hadn't spent time together in person in months. Only this rock-solid of a friendship could survive some of the fights we easily slipped into in the years leading up to this drive and during the drive itself. On the road, we also argued about how to pump gas, whether the headlights were on (and, if not, which switch would turn them on), how to defog the windshield. We don't always like each other, but the unconditionality of her love has been one of the few things I've been able to stay sure of in my unpredictable and loss-heavy life. This was a journey with family to visit more family, and when she wasn't napping or taking calls, we had plenty of time to discuss the distress that came with our impressive-sounding day job titles, and how taken aback we were about not being more settled by then. How we sometimes wish we had gone down a more traditional path and had focused on family planning well before hitting 35. How expensive everything had become, financially and otherwise. It all seemed so pathetically and per-

---

on a hill. And drove the streets beautifully, immediately afterwards. I have never hit a person or an animal.

manently chaotic until we drove into the most gorgeous multicolored sunset I'd ever seen, right after crossing the Ohio border. As Fleetwood Mac's "Silver Springs" softly played in the background, the thought of every big decision either of us had made up to that point, and every consequence it created, gave me a sense of fullness, like I'd just slowly eaten an enormous but simple meal that had been prepared with careful tenderness.

***

A couple of days after driving home, I insisted on chauffeuring my dad to one of his cemetery visits, where he lights candles at my mom's and other relatives' gravesites. By this point, I had dozens upon dozens of hours of driving experience all through the rough-and-tumble island of Manhattan, and passed a Monday morning rush hour road test in the Boogie Down Bronx. I had just driven almost 12 hours across three different state lines. As we buckled up and I started the car, in a huge rush to get to the cemetery before it closed, my dad and I both assumed I'd no longer have any problem backing out of my family compound's driveway.

Professional driving schools train student-customers for their particular region's road test. In New York, passing the road test involves driving around the city streets, parallel parking, and doing a broken U-turn. No one had ever trained me on how best to drive backwards all the way down a narrow, partially winding strip with a suburban house on each side. I spent close to five minutes trying, running over a bed of pretty flowers in the process.

"You almost hit my house," my dad said after he got out of the car to survey the damage to his gardening efforts, before ejecting me from the driver's seat and taking over, until he pulled over farther down our tree-lined street, and we switched places again. The round-trip drive to the cemetery was excruciating, teleporting me to teenagedom and the sheer hell of driving with my parents, made to feel like everything I did was wide off the mark, even when it wasn't. He forbade me from going one mile over the speed limit, as all the other cars calmly and graciously (there's no place like the Midwest) passed me. While I slowly made a turn, he barked out "GO!" As soon as I went more quickly, he theatrically read me the riot act midway through the turn, now declaring it too fast. This is how accidents happen. The difference between my confidence level at 16 versus 36 was that I no longer took everything my elders, no matter who they are, told me to heart. I have a more fine-tuned sense of which parts to listen to and which to ignore. "You're lucky you got this extra training in with me today," my closest elder said, smirking while shaking his head when we returned to the house without any physical bruising.

On the morning I left to pick Rhonda up at her brother's place before we headed back to New York, I asked my dad to repeat his recent advice about what to do with the brakes if we drove into heavy rain, to avoid hydroplaning. I listened to his instructions. "But you'll be OK," he said with a smile so sincere I believed it too. Especially since, 10 minutes earlier, he'd backed the rental SUV out of the driveway and parked it on the street in front of our house, allowing me to pull out from the curb, the way we do it in NYC.

POTENTIALLY PRIVILEGED

The morning after one of the region's most brazen winter storms in at least a year, my job interview with the president of a specialized cruise line still hadn't been canceled. I showed up at his Upper East Side townhouse as scheduled that afternoon, gliding on sheets of ice and climbing over roadside snow mounds in black patent leather flats that I still wear today. All this for a copywriter position when I didn't necessarily want to work as a copywriter.

Wow, did *el presidente* and I click. It was much more of a conversation than an interview, like chatting and catching up with a dear childhood friend's dad. He asked why I responded to this particular job advertisement and I might have gone on about how I've always loved to write and the written word, and how I'd always felt more comfortable with writing than with speaking, running down the list of my experiences and supplementary skill sets. I thought I had this thing in the bag. Until his tone shifted and he declared that I needed to set my sights higher than applying for copywriting positions at outfits like his. "I see you running a foundation," he added, followed by a lecture on how there's no greater tragedy than wasted talent.

Such an inspiring pep talk would make for a cool story if he—someone with contacts, influence, seemingly effusive faith in me—proceeded to do something, anything, to help. But he didn't. Didn't invite me to an event, refer me to others, become a mentor. His preferred role was more along the lines of, "Now off you go, and good luck!" as he became one more potentially useful connection I didn't have.

They say it takes the average job seeker three to six months to find a new position. Here's a snapshot of my own job-searching prowess: it took me eight months to land an entry-level salaried position in my chosen field, a little more than two years to find a mid-level salaried position, and eight years to find a senior-level salaried slot. There are many able-bodied, college-educated members of society whose attempts at finding gainful employment can be summed up as bungling at best. I've come to terms with the fact that I'm one of them.

My personal definition of gainful employment goes a little something like this: a career-track job that pays much more than the amount of your regular living expenses, provides an option for longevity, offers an array of employee benefits, *and* the idea of which doesn't make you shudder to the point of waking in the middle of the night in a heart-racing, butterflies-in-stomach panic more than once a month. In novels and magazine profiles, other people just get or take jobs, the way I get or take menus from Asian fusion restaurants within my delivery zone. "KiKi moved to San Francisco and took a job as the program manager at a nonprofit." "After months of waiting tables during the afternoons and smoking up every night, Derrick got a job as the athletics operations manager at a Catholic high school, five blocks away from the club he still frequented." When I see the date ranges of other people's résumés, they're so linear. One full-time salaried job ends in February 2010 and the next (noticeably better) one starts the same month or one month later. Whereas my trajectory features a wee bit more zigzagging.

***

They also say you should never leave a full-time salaried job without having another full-time salaried job lined up, and they're right. It's the advice I'd give almost anyone who asked, because I've done it twice. You may have statement necklaces or a statement shirt. I've had statement resignations. The first time, I was barely making enough money to comfortably live off of, often had weekend work to take home, and belonged to a department that did not promote all of the performers in a timely manner. Even if I did get promoted to the next rung of that ladder, my annual salary would have gone from $32,000 to something like $35,000. Still not enough for someone in her twenties, living in New York with student loan debt, who didn't come from or marry into money.

After putting in more than two years as an editorial assistant (the last year of which I spent looking for anything amounting to a step up), I gave two weeks' notice and easily lined up a full-time temp job across town. For the next 14 months or so, I led a colorful short-term work life, while continuing my real job search for something with the word "editor," but not "assistant," in its title. I temped for an internationally focused nonprofit, an old boys' network corporation, and a small business that found work for those job searching in other countries. I freelance wrote/consulted for a delightful divorcée in her swanky apartment (there was a housekeeper who wore an actual old-school maid's uniform) in a doorman building across the street from Central Park. I also worked as her personal assistant, with duties including buying underwear and shoe insoles for her adult daughter. All of this until I finally found new full-time salaried work, right around the time when a catastrophic financial crisis, leading up to the Great Recession, kicked off.

***

I couldn't have been more thrilled about advancing to my mid-level role. I now had a proper office (with a door that closed and locked, and a view of both 30 Rock and my old office building) instead of a cubicle. After my first couple of direct deposit pay periods, I was baffled by all the extra money I saw in my checking account balance. I thought my landlord might not have received my rent checks or I'd somehow forgotten to pay several bills, until it sank in that this is what it meant to really have disposable income. I vowed to never again leave a full-time salaried job without having formally accepted another one. No more maverick pridefulness, I was now pushing 30, far too old and wise for quirky experimentation. I kept up with that promise for years.

The problem was that I now worked with Babs, someone who outranked me at this enormous organization. Without getting into the details, suffice it to say that this is the only person I've ever had regular contact with who has made me feel unsafe and intensely on guard. "You really haven't done yourself any favors with this," she once said to me, with a Disney cartoon-villain glint in her eyes, in response to my having corrected three statements she wrote in a memo arising from our most recent source of conflict.

"You won't be at a place like that for long," one of the greatest people I worked under during drifting period #1 said, early on in my tenure at this office. "A year from now, you'll be out of there, off doing something better."

I searched for a new and improved editorial job almost every day, sending out résumés in response to compelling online postings. One year passed, and then another. I barely got interviews. When I did manage to get an interview, as well as most went, I didn't get the job. I reached out to headhunters and joined LinkedIn. I read social media posts that provided job-hunting tips like: (1) Get Going; (2) Set Goals; (3) Spend Time with Positive People; (4) Find an Accountability Partner.

Midway through Year Three of this, I was stunned. Maybe my salary requirements were too high. Maybe these prospective employers thought my résumé came off as too free-spirited and saw me as a flight risk, maybe too many hiring managers googled me and didn't like the cheeky tone of some of my writing that was out there, maybe they had a problem with the way I look. Maybe all of this, none of it, or more. I was almost exclusively using job boards, which conventional wisdom says is the least successful way to go. So many people seemed to make their next professional moves through personal contacts and networking.

I've never been good at networking. I never made the "right" connections or an effort to stay in touch with the "right" people. I approach large gatherings more journalistically than participationally. I'm an introvert, sociable but not a social butterfly, and networking feels awkward, enervating, and like using people. Not only don't I choose or maintain relationships based on what the other person can do for me, most people I'm naturally drawn to tend to have far less "social capital" and fewer resources than I do. This price I paid was a little too steep for my liking.

***

Hardly anybody I knew (including those who did what they could to help me) profusely pitied me. It's a job that looked amazing on paper—the title and responsibilities, the overall cause, the amount of paid leave time, a job "some would kill for," I was told. Since I couldn't find another equally good or better position that paid as much, I tried making the most of where I was. I volunteered as an on-site writing tutor. I co-chaired the office birthday club, for God's sake—me, someone who never so much as considered rushing a sorority! Outside of work, I created a blog and began building this book, to keep myself artistically fulfilled. I paid off all my commercial debt and a huge chunk of my student loans. I took trips to places I'd always wanted to visit but hadn't been able to afford.

Speaking of going places, Babs—who had started to generally back off, from me at least, for long stretches of time—was transferred to another division for six months! That became one of the most stimulating and rewarding half-years of my career. But she eventually returned, and things got really bad again, for months. Not every single day of those months, but enough to make it all unsustainable. If I'd had a kid or someone else to financially support, my attitude may have been different. I may have put up with this for much longer, possibly until retirement. But, in that era, I was in charge of looking after only my own well-being, and the longer I stayed, the lower my personal peace, the more I had to cleanse my aura, the whole nine yards.

For the second time within a 10-year period, I quit my steady day job, giving two-weeks' notice, after making sure I had about four months' worth of savings and lining up one multi-project freelance client, entering into drifting period #2, still some years away from 40. I would editorially freelance until someone hired me for a new and senior-level salaried position. A major national recession had ended and, as my retirement fund's phone representative said after I called to confirm that my 401K could stay put, I was still "relatively young."

A few months after quitting, I still had no new job. And no new freelancing projects. I needed to come up with another lucrative source of income, fast, as I had quite a lifestyle to maintain. In the years since my last drifting period, my rent was almost twice as high, I had HBO and high-speed internet service to pay for, and now had to buy health insurance to avoid future tax penalties.

Three of the things I hated most in this world were the legal profession, asking people for money, and talking on the phone. So I took on two new gigs—one as a contract "attorney" (more commonly known, to those of us with law degrees, as doc review)[13] and the other working in a call center as a tele-fundraiser. The doc review was the lucrative income source. The call-center earnings were supplemental. After weeks of no luck finding even short-term work, this call center was the first place to offer me something, and I couldn't wait to get out of the house and report to a bona fide workplace after four months of sitting alone in my apartment most of each weekday. In a matter of months, I'd gone from a well-paying full-time workplace

---

[13] I never ended up taking the bar exam or getting licensed to practice law, but many of those I temped with during this drifting period did.

where there weren't many rules to a low-paying part-time workplace that set and enforced as many rules as they could think of. While on call-center premises I couldn't have my cell phone out, clock in more than 10 minutes before a shift began, chit-chat too much while packing up to leave at the end of the night. Most of my fellow callers were either artists or might as well have been—sculptors, actors, musicians, comedians, a Weather Underground alum, a Black guy in an online rabbinical school program, graduates of Juilliard and Columbia, recovering addicts, a former HBO casting director who spent summer weekends in the Hamptons. Colleagues who said things to me like, "Can we stay in touch? You're good for my act." After more than a decade in New York City, I had to get rerouted here to fall in with the alternative cool people.

**

For about a year, I became more of a professional doc reviewer than an editor (many months, any freelancing earnings amounted to nothing more than extra pocket change), spending up to 60 hours a week in a computer lab, coding documents (for example, was the communication Responsive, Potentially Privileged, or Not Privileged?) from the parties involved in a lawsuit's work-email accounts, the often-snarky content of which made me miss having a real job. I worked until 6 p.m. one New Year's Eve, ecstatic about the opportunity to earn more money. If a project went into overtime hours, I could earn two months' rent in three weeks. For two months, I worked two on-site gigs at once, six or seven days a week, five or six days at doc review from 9 a.m. until 4:45 p.m., then running across town a few nights a week to make my 5 p.m. to 9 p.m. shift at the call center. When another doc reviewer asked what second job I dashed off to, I referred to it as political fundraising (by that time, I'd pulled in around five grand for left-wing causes), leaving out the call center or minimum wage (plus commission) parts. I mulled over text from freelance clients, in between reviewing documents, during 11-hour shifts. With my non-linear credentials and go-getter drive, I had options, lots of them, too many, in fact, anointing me more potentially privileged than the documents I reviewed. While first getting to know a call-center artist, as we chatted while dialing and mostly getting people's voicemails, she asked whether there was anything I hadn't tried that I wish I had, and I said not really. I've tried, was in the act of trying, or was about to try pretty much everything that's seemed important to me.

Financially, some months were decent, others were great, and some months I barely scraped by. I still persistently looked for salaried work in my field, while trying to avoid spending the money running out of my bank accounts. I read posts in the comments section of more than one website insisting how easy women of color have it in the hiring process, that we don't even need to prove we're smart or qualified. I met with a career coach. I "visualized" and "believed I deserved" success and "practiced affirmations," per spiritual sages' advice. "Maybe you're not someone who's meant to have a full-time job," one suggested.

Less than a year after my most recent resignation, my savings/emergency account was depleted, and I faced months when, two weeks before the rent was due, I realized I wouldn't have enough in my checking account to pay it on time, even though I had been doggedly working in the weeks prior. (Freelancers often have to chase down checks from clients. Some institutions have net-45 payment terms, meaning I would have to wait more than a month after my invoice date to receive the money. Some of the doc review agencies paid biweekly instead of weekly. Three paychecks got lost in the mail, requiring additional waiting for replacement checks.) Someone I know gave me a couple of opportunities to earn enough extra money doing work (anything from editing annual reports to executing labor-intensive mass mailings) for the small community organization she ran, in order to get the rent paid punctually. A few times, someone else gave me temporary loans until the money I had earned and was waiting for finally arrived. In my teens and early twenties, I'd worked my ass off to avoid being in this exact position, under the impression that if you worked hard and went to a great college, the rest of your résumé-oriented life would be a stroll through a botanical garden, as long as you delivered shining performances. Nobody had warned me that credentials without connections are like cups of coffee without caffeine—utterly useless when it's time to efficiently get things done.

As exhausted, concerned, and blindsided about my future as I was, I was calmer and sprightlier than I'd been in years. I drank less and slept more soundly. As long as I had my health and sense of humor, I'd be OK. During one call-center-shift conversation, the guy next to me mentioned that he never figured me for a drinker. I wonder whether he'd have said the same thing if he'd known me (and my bloodshot eyes) while I still worked with Babs. By my third year with her, I drank heavily at least four nights a week, most weeks. A few months before entering drifting period #2, I started seeing a therapist, in dire need of a neutral, expert sounding board. I could only afford to continue seeing her for about two months after the resignation. In one of those final sessions, I thought aloud about how my life could be easier if I simply surrendered more. Maybe I mishandled the Babs nightmare and should have just bowed down, sucked up, and powered through, giving her what she wanted (more enthusiasm and less disengagement, pretending that I found her more marvelous than malevolent), while collecting a comfortable paycheck and enviable benefits. The therapist immediately, emphatically, shook her head as she said, "But that's not who you are."

***

I was at doc review when I got the offer for the new full-time job I'd spent almost a decade searching for. I negotiated my salary from a cramped hallway, a floor above the cramped review room. Not long after my triumphant return to the salaried scene, during a walking-tour portion of a team retreat, my new co-workers and I strolled past that doc review building. I didn't say a word. Once again, my life had dramatically changed, on paper, in a matter of weeks.

That upgraded role was like finding my Prince Charming (by the way, I scored this upgrade solely off of an online job board—no networking, no connections—something I'd essentially been told only happened in fairy tales). As much of an improvement as this was (for starters, less than a year in, I got blessed with a boss who was more like a fairy godmother than a higher-up), it wasn't long before I was open to looking for something that might make me happier, since I was still "relatively young." If it wasn't the money, it was the people. If it wasn't the people, it was the nature of the work. If it wasn't the nature of the work, it was the hours. In so many ways, I have been a professional and perennial searcher at heart and by trade, honing the (marketable?) skill of gradually upgrading the quality of my daily life for a living. Marketability is a state of mind. And if steadily upgrading the quality of one's daily life isn't an art form, I don't know what is.

THIS IS NOT A LULLABY

There was a time (a long time, way more than a few years, off and on) when I couldn't really sleep in New York. Not most nights. Not the deep, rejuvenating sort of sleep we're supposed to lie down and take to. This is slightly more of a fact than a complaint.

Outside of planes, trains, or automobiles, I could fall and stay asleep pretty much everywhere else. In the homes of loved ones living in other cities and towns. In other cities' and towns' hotels and motels. What kept me up in New York, my headquarters, where I lived, worked, and played? Well, the sounds of the city—sputtering radiators, wailing sirens, sustained honking, construction crews' early-morning jackhammering, noise from the apartments of neighbors who lived ONE BUILDING OVER—didn't help. More importantly, New York was *my headquarters, where I lived, worked, and played.* Where it's harder to skate away from the bigger anxieties that can plague people of certain age brackets or stations in life: How could I have said and done those things I'm not proud of when I was younger? When would I become completely free of student loan debt? Could I land a lucrative day job that didn't eventually dampen my spirits? Would I ever graduate from home-renter to home-owner, or should I even want to? How much longer until I meet this elusive love of my life, the without? By then, would I have enough good eggs left to conceive? Why did I have that sex dream about someone I can't stand during my waking hours? Does that mean *he's* the top prize, is that how this works? The questioning went on and on, for hours.

Caffeine wasn't the culprit—on the days I drank coffee, it was usually no more than two cups and rarely after 2 p.m. I hardly led a sedentary life—most days, I got between one and three hours of brisk cardio. Sipping wine left me wired, not tired. I tried dabbing lavender oil on my pillowcase and all it did was leave a stain. Earplugs sometimes helped me get five hours of sleep instead of three. Instead of waking at 5 a.m., I often dozed off at 5 a.m., rolling with it, owning it, occasionally reveling in it. It's kind of cool to be wide awake when the average person in your time zone is not, every action or inaction seeming more profound. Very Rolling Stones or Tupac Shakur during their prolific songwriting and touring heydays, and excellent practice for future parenthood, this aptitude for proficiently, if not optimally, functioning on days of four-hours-of-sleep nights. (Bill Clinton does it, or at least he used to. I might have first read about that one in the middle of the night, too.) The late-night hours, when I'm officially off-duty, are quieter, more relaxed, and raw. My mind is in its fullest form when I'm coming off an entire day of happenings that remind me of past happenings and give me ideas about what could still happen. I love walking home up Broadway or across 125th Street after midnight, when the pedestrians are fewer and less guarded. I'm not afraid of the dark.

Proponents of fasting maintain that food deprivation heightens their senses to the point of fueling epiphanies, their heady moments of clarity. That's what this particular sleeping shortage once did for me. This book you're reading, the books I've read, some of the wisest decisions I've made; I owe my chronic anxiety a personalized thank-you card. I have had more minutes to play with, more chances to take, more time to reflect than the habitually sound sleepers. There was also my robust immune system (I went almost eight years without coming down with so much as the sniffles) and the reality that, contrary to prevailing dietetics research, I probably lost more weight than I gained during those years, in no small part due to the core-strengthening moves I picked up from overnight Hip Hop Abs infomercials. Some believe that an inability to fall asleep means you're awake in someone else's dreams—how flattering to imagine myself factoring into that many people's enchanted headspaces, all night long.

Still, I'm the first to admit it: New York City and I needed a solid nap. No power napping, something heartier and more humbling. I'd been receptive to the idea of getting help. I stayed clear of the internet, the TV, and my phone an hour before my preferred bedtime. Although I'm not sure I did it correctly, I meditated. Years earlier, I tried prescription sleeping pills a couple of times and the throbbing headaches that came with them yanked me into a closed-eyed vacuum I feared I wouldn't wake up from. It was time for a foolproof fix that wouldn't involve drugs, hypnosis, white-noise machines, weighted blankets, or too much open judgment from the people whose opinions I cared about.

**

Vermont is one of my happy places, where my mind and body are released on parole. Pleasant townsfolk, stately scenery, progressive values, live and let live. When my mom's family moved to this country as refugees, central Vermont took them in first, and her revisiting of those initial US stomping grounds decades later remains one of my most idyllic family vacation memories. I've spent a fair amount of time in Vermont since then, and it's one spot where I consistently *have* been able to get in some routine sleeping, even after accepting a 5:30 p.m. sip-while-you-browse cappuccino from the owner of an authentically bohemian boutique, where there are no funky attitudes, nobody's looking people up and down by way of comparison, and there's no slavishness to the principal fads. Hippies > Hipsters.

Before leaving the mountains to return to the city, I used to stop into the nearest food co-op catering to the locavore demographic to stock up on tofu sushi, organic apple butter, loaves of cheddar-and-onion *focaccia*, real maple syrup, purple tin water bottles with butterflies etched onto them. *Here's another reason I need to move up here*, I used to think while loitering through every last aisle, ogling bins of seeds and containers of bee pollen. *I can't get this wide of a selection of free-spirit fare all in one location from an independent distributor in my quadrant of Manhattan.*

As it turned out, I'd long been living two blocks away from a health food store that was a smaller, surlier, pricier, and danker (a retail iteration of an urban starter apartment) spin on the Vermont emporiums. I went in there one night after having read some encouraging literature about using valerian tea, a natural tranquilizer, as a sleep aid. A non-pharmaceutical alternative to Valium ("mother's little helper"), its sedative effect is rumored to help with both insomnia and hysteria. As a daughter in need of some help, I bought a 24-count box of valerian tea bags, to the tune of more than $8. Warning labels on the side of the box read: "Do not use when driving a motor vehicle or operating machinery" and "Not for those under the age of 18." Perfect.

I take care of my own. The next morning, I dropped four bags of V into a Ziploc baggie and brought it to work with me so a co-worker could take it home to her sleep-challenged husband. The stench wafted terribly out of my handbag, latching onto that side of my jacket for the rest of the day. Imagine how a pair of thick, cheap athletic socks would smell immediately after a burly man completed a rain-soaked triathlon in them. And that, during this race, there had been a couple of holes in each sneaker, allowing muddy rainwater to come on in. Now, to that, add a pungent licorice-y (not as sweet as Twizzlers or Red Vines) tang. That's the aroma of these tea bags, especially when there's more than one bag around at a time. Of course, the co-worker was out sick that day. I stored the baggie in a desk drawer, and by early afternoon my entire office reeked of V. When I walked through the cold outdoor air during lunchtime, I smelled it there too, attached to my clothing, possibly seeped into my skin. "Valere" is Latin for "to be strong," something I intend to excel at.

My mom, another night owl and member of the sleep-challenged caste (she has said that when she nodded off while reading children's books to me, I would turn around, reach up, and pry her eyes back open with my fingers), once advised me to surrender to sleep whenever I finally did feel legitimately tired, no matter what time of day it was, to catch up on rest when I could. When you're in a meeting or at an engagement party, this suggestion gets compli-cated. But I generally follow it, which is why I have spent so many weekend mornings and afternoons comatose in my bed, after days of running on fewer than six hours of decent shut-eye. When, in the past, I've woken up in an unrelenting daze at 9 a.m. on a Sunday morning and de-cided to bail out of non-essential plans so I can go back to bed and reawaken refreshed four hours later, there's no chance I missed out on anything better.

***

Tea drinking is such an elegant, genteel ritual. My dear grandmother drank tons of Lipton and Tetley. I never hated tea, but rarely have had the instinct to reach for it in lieu of something, anything, else. From an early age, I've noticed some differences between the tea and coffee fiends. Devout tea drinkers usually don't have that wild look in their eyes and tend not to interrupt or dart in front of others as much. They're more scrupulous about using their indoor voices, and when they speak, their listeners don't say, "Slow down, you sound like a machine gun!" They know how to keep the fidgeting under control. They neither curse unnecessarily nor chomp, crack, or blow bubbles with their gum. They're more likely to appreciate fine china and wear slippers around the house. After seeing additional text on my tea bag box, alluding to the many health benefits and herbal healing properties of the valerian root, ideas about investing in a set of saucers flew around inside my head.

Sure enough, as soon as I drank my first cup of V, I felt altered, enhanced. My bloodstream entered the beginning stages of a deep cleanse, although it could have been a placebo, like so much is. After a few sips of my second cup, there was no sign of drowsiness, only amplified anticipation. I was ready to end the high-adrenaline party in my nerves and make a tea bag-popper out of me. But what was taking so long?

I googled how much I'd need to drink to be sedated and found a few websites suggesting it would take four or five bags (it's a milligram thing) to get the effect of one Valium. That's a lot of tea for a coffee drinker, especially when it's tea that doesn't taste like rosé or smell like roses.

I wouldn't even dare drink five coffees in one day. The handful of times I have, I was drafting haikus and doing push-ups at 4 a.m., trying to ignore every heart palpitation. Heart palpitations and overdoing it with the caffeine take me back to the first few months of college, where I developed the taste for coffee, following the lead of the girl next door. Since she, a worldly New England boarding school graduate, ordered caramel macchiatos at campus cafés, so did I. By the end of that year, I gained more than the Freshman 15 and she didn't.

To speed up the sedation, I plopped an extra bag of V into my partially finished second cup. If you ever want to keep your sweet little nine-year-olds from saying things like, "fuck this" or "I hate you and your wack rules," forget about time-outs, withholding electronics, or washing mouths out with soap. Just put a double-bagged cup of valerian tea in front of them and demand that they drink it. Set them up at a table and insist they're forbidden from continuing on with any facet of their lives until the cup is *drained*. They'll never act up in your presence again.

That night, I cut myself off after a total of two cups, three bags—a little more than half a Valium tablet. When I looked at the clock, the time was 1:15 a.m. I was still headbanging and twirling around to electropop beats on the radio. And really needed to go to the bathroom, then and for the rest of the night/morning.

When one of my aunts stayed at my house during my teenage years, I overheard her put my little cousin down to bed, continuously referring to bedtime as "Nighttime-Sleeptime." The type of overnight refuge they cooed about made a good night's sleep sound like an honor bestowed on the angelic ones. Years later, when I sincerely wanted to conk out but couldn't, the Nighttime-Sleeptime concept semi-haunted me. *I'm not that kind of angel*, I thought, *not anymore, not yet, or maybe I never really was.* I was willing to settle for a third- or fourth-best retreat, which is what I assumed V would upgrade me to. V had all the makings of a savior, I was sure of it. Some of the world's biggest cynics are the most stubborn optimists. Translation: it wasn't over yet. I concluded I must have high valerian tolerance. I'd just need to drink more than the standard person to lock in a suitable anti-buzz, to numb down.

***

My revised plan was simple: I would set aside an entire evening for rigorous, uninterrupted experimentation, binge drinking bag after bag to see how many it would take to knock me out. After I determined my ballpark number, I'd go back to the health food store and buy another box to keep on hand strictly for emergencies, for that occasional night when my nerves were particularly, intolerably strung out. For those nights that followed days that brought bad news or news too good to be true. Or, worst of all, for those nights when there was no pinpointable reason why I couldn't sleep, as I tossed around and stared out into the darkness, thinking of nothing at all—these were the cheer-less stretches of time that de-romanticized insomnia.

On the weeknight I devoted to the operation, the trial began at 6 p.m. Over the course of four hours, I drank five cups, five bags. I snacked on cheese, bananas, whole grains, and other foods I already regularly ate that purportedly ease the falling-asleep process. Where was the placebo? I had, for the first time in months, the urge to head out for a three-mile run. I didn't act on it but should have because another long night loomed ahead and my clothes weren't getting any looser. Two mornings later, I woke up with half a sore throat.

The two times I've had oral surgery, the anesthesia took me to the other side without a hitch, and I fell in love with each experience, slipping into unconsciousness or under-consciousness[14] slowly at first, then with a painless boom. That's what I told myself the valerian would do for me, and I couldn't wait for its magical powers to take effect. What does it mean if a tranquilizer has the reverse effect on you? I returned to Google to get as close to an answer as possible, in writing. This information popped up:

> [Valerian] does not work like the over-the-coun-ter drugs that will "knock you out" [my own hopeful words!] for the night. Typically, it will

---

[14] The first time, the dentist, oral surgeon, or whoever he was introduced me to "the twilight zone" (this was even better than it sounds), during which you're technically still awake.

take several days or even weeks of consumption
before an individual is able to see any results.[15]

A bomb that should have been dropped on the side of the tea bag box, where there was plenty of room for more copy. Although delayed gratification has its times and places, I wouldn't allow this to be one of them. I was interested in sleep, it just wasn't that into me. I found it completely unreliable, passing me up and handling me like an afterthought, a fling, instead of the way I deserved to be treated. Nobody should have to work this hard or drink this much to chill out. There I was, back at Square One, a setting from which I never seem gone for long.

***

When I checked out a library book about sleep's fundamental, often overlooked importance to our overall well-being, it came with a pair of turquoise earplugs (my own earplugs have been beige, lavender, hot pink) stuck between two of its opening pages. I pressed down on each plug and the foam rapidly rose, like loaves of maniacally baking bread. This means they had only been used once, twice, or not at all, the soft and colorful detritus of another hopeful, heavy-eyed local taking that, "Anything is possible in New York!" propaganda to heart.

---

[15] See, for example, https://www.dailyhealthmagazine.com/valerian-root-benefits.

Earplugs or no earplugs, I figured I'd grow sleepier with age, assuming this age would more likely be sometime in my sixties than sometime in my thirties. I first suspected I had a medical malfunction when I kept gaining weight for no reason, and my second clue involved feeling cold all the time in spite of the extra padding. Clue #3 came by way of all the sleeping I started to do. When I wasn't sleeping or lying down, all I thought about was sleeping or lying down. I slept through the night. I fell into bed at 10 p.m. and woke at 8 a.m., still worn out and swollen-eyed, trudging along in a fog all day, after three cups of coffee. My doctor tentatively diagnosed me with an autoimmune disorder, eventually referring me to an endocrinologist who confirmed I have Hashimoto's disease, or autoimmune thyroiditis. You don't see too many 5K races or walkathons on behalf of this one.

This minor (for me) and manageable (so far) condition has adjusted my lifestyle. I now have much healthier eating habits. I exercise, focusing on both cardio and strength, without over-exercising. Most nights, I absolutely need eight or nine hours of uninterrupted sleep. I don't always get it,[16] this has just become my new standard, something else to actively strive toward, possibly one of the most important long-term goals I've set yet. A psychic once told me I'd live until 100, and that she didn't really see any

---

[16] The valerian tea experiment (the very need for it) took place more than a year after my first Hashimoto's flare-up.

grave physical problems in store for me—just a lot of emotional ones, unless I found a way to curb the "nervousness."

Now that I'm more of a sleeper, part of me feels less productive. For those of us with Type A personalities, productivity (the sheer aura of it) is essential to self-worth. Sometimes it seems like all we have. Driven, multi-tasking, results-oriented (Google and I came up with the Hashimoto's likelihood long before the doctors did), hard on other people, so much harder on ourselves. That was my overarching identity. It still is, but identities can be toned down and classed up. Although many of my big-picture anxieties have barely abated, the better-rested version of myself can handle them less frenetically. More sleeping has helped my mind and output become more thoughtful and effective.

More sleeping has also brought on more dreaming. (As it all comes full circle, roughly how many others have now lost sleep due to these unexpected improvements on my end? Sometimes as many as 10 people from my past or present make vivid appearances in my dreams on one night alone.) I used to look down on overnight or naptime dreams because they weren't real or realistic, they taunted and teased. But not only can dreamers double as doers, is there any better gift than having a nightmare and waking up to realize it's not true, that you have the chance to turn certain scenarios around? That half your teeth didn't fall out or someone you love actually hadn't ditched you for another? That you didn't fall out of a private jet into the ocean below and have to swim against the current to safety while everyone on shore pointed and laughed? That you never crawled into a dingy, doorless roadside vintage shop only to be told it carries nothing but children's items (and you never walked around the aisles, just to be nice, unsuccessfully haggling the cashier-owner to come down from $3 to $2 for a ratty pop-up book, right before a strap of your tote bag broke)? That you didn't wake up any worse off than you'd been eight hours earlier? That you are still as alive as ever?

A PET ISSUE

Chinese zodiac-wise, I was born the Year of the Horse, and it shows. One of my favorite New York moments unfolded as I waited to cross a street, standing a few yards away from a carriage horse parked on Central Park South. After some meaningful eye contact, the horse suddenly, dramatically, walked toward me, pulling the unmanned carriage behind him, to come pay his respects. An act so poignant and out of place with its surroundings, I won't hesitate to describe it as semi-biblical. "He's just looking for food," the astounded off-duty driver said (gawking at me as if I were about to hand out a hex before flying off on a broomstick), as the horse rested his (he looked like a Tommy or a Trey) head on my shoulder while I kissed his nose and stroked his head. When the light turned green, neither of us noticed.

I'd had my eye on these carriage horses, a longtime tourist attraction (in New York as well as in other urban centers), for months, unsure of what to do, or how. I've signed petitions and taken to social media. I attended a cash-bar fundraiser catered by the vegans. I voted for former mayor Bill de Blasio, who made a campaign promise to get these horses off New York City streets, once and for all. As of this writing, the horses are still there. They look fed but starving for more. Tough but self-conscious. Reluctant survivors, displaying more humanity than more than a few humans I've known. Emotionally broken down but awake, ready to run, smart enough to wait until they get the timing right. It's unsettling to walk or drive past them in and around Central Park, which is something I did on a regular basis (sometimes twice a day) for years. Their drivers have them making sudden U-turns and complicated left-hand turning maneuvers onto Broadway during after-dark evening rush hour. They have been legally permitted to work at least eight hours a day, seven days a week, on concrete, even when inside the park. When I hear the defenders of the carriage horse industry insist their horses are well cared for, it's not unlike watching *Annie* and listening to Miss Hannigan imply those orphanage girls were in good hands, as healthy as horses.

All animals are my spirit animals. They provide me with invaluable emotional support, and I haven't come across many who I haven't loved unconditionally. I kiss their asses, connect more naturally with four-legged furry beings than with people, and don't need to complete a certification program to cement my reputation as an animal communicator. I'm not a cat person or a dog person, I'm an animal person, and was one of those girls who became infatuated with horses, fully mesmerized by their strength and majesty, those eyes and thick tails. I grew up with pets, there was usually one dog and two cats in the house, and I don't consider a house a full-blown home unless and until there's at least one furry soul living there around the clock. I have bonded with raccoons and own a ring with the image of an elk's head on its face. I resent all who hunt and fish for sport, and those who wear real fur. One line I've tucked into the longtime bucket list I keep toward the end of my personal journal reads: "Hug a monkey, preferably a chimpanzee."

After a delicious meat-and-potatoes-fueled midwestern childhood, I've wished I had the willpower for full-time vegetarianism, purely out of solidarity with my real tribe. When I went away to college, I missed my dog and cats more than I missed any of the human beings who remained an easy phone call or email away. Zoom, Skype, Google Hangouts, and FaceTime didn't exist back then, and even if they did, my wordless kindred spirits would have hated those video calls more than I do.

The pediatric urgent care center around the corner from my old apartment used to be a *bodega*, where a huge black cat named Moose roamed the aisles. I would stroll in there, often buying nothing, just to spend time with her. We couldn't get enough of each other. As soon as I plopped down on the store's dirty floor, she scampered into my lap, purring as I pet her as we both entered a meditative state. The guy who ran the place eventually offered her to me and I wavered. A few months later, she was gone, awarded to someone who hadn't. I blinked because I've refused to adopt a dog or cat of my own until I'm able or willing to arrange for a sitter, because I've known that not having a sitter would downgrade me to having literally no life. I would cater to the dog's or cat's every outrageous whim. A 17-day house/cat-sitting stint in New Jersey confirmed these suspicions. At work and while commuting on the train that month, I worried about how the cat (we'll call him Santino, to protect his privacy) was feeling, what he was doing, whether he felt abandoned or bored, the sounds of his anguished or angry meowing echoing in my head. This one-year-old cat was more like a dog than a cat. He gave big kisses, actually puckering up and planting them on you. He often sprinted to the door to greet me when I walked into the house after more than a few hours away. I slept in heavenly peace with this cat. I got irregular sores on the insides of my lips from this cat. When I couldn't figure out how to reset the living room and bedroom light timers, I raced home earlier than I needed to so Santino wouldn't have to sit alone in the dark, like a downcast millennial not used to rejection who has just been passed over for a promotion at his event planning agency in the city. In my final caretaking days with him that month, I hoped and dreamed there would be enough of a problem with my friends' return flight to allow me to extend my stay. Not all my prayers get answered.

***

When we were growing up, my best friend Kristen and I talked our parents into sending us to a two-week horse camp, a full-time summer day camp, on a small farm in a neighboring suburb, on the other side of some railroad tracks. In the rare moments we weren't lolling around in my basement or on my front porch, Kristen and I happened to pursue a number of extracurricular, non-school-based activities and lessons together. There was a pottery workshop and a sign language class. Well, I guess that's just two, not counting the horseback riding, although we did, over the course of several days, quite seriously look into karate training. You get the idea; anything that wasn't a team sport. She's three years younger than me, so we weren't in the same grade. But she lived three houses down the street, and not only were we virtually inseparable, it often felt as though we lived in our own special, private world. A more enthralling and better-off world, enhanced by convenience-store junk food; unconventional inside jokes; notorious cackling outbursts; and divulging innermost secrets, fears, and politically incorrect opinions. There was a subtle, semi-sociable us-versus-them mentality I wouldn't have traded in for anything else. So pretty much everyone at this camp hated us (same goes for the pottery and sign language folks, not to mention at least a couple of our neighbors). Neither of us would have made it all the way through a sleepaway camp if we couldn't have done so as a duet.

In the immediate post-camp years, I referred to the experience as an equestrian camp. But just plain "horse camp" was this program's official name, which was more fitting, as nothing about it was on the higher end of any spectrum. We wore no jackets or elegant boots, and I had no idea what jodhpurs actually were until watching a late-2000s episode of *The Real Housewives of DC*. Every lunch break, one camper drank Mountain Dew straight from a two-liter plastic green bottle. We did things like consent to getting herded into the back of a van for a bumpy ride around the farm's block to "see how the horses feel" when they traveled. It remains one of the most fabulous and formative shitshows I've been a part of. The grooming and other caregiving roles (refilling water buckets, brushing manes and tails, curry-combing and washing the horses' bodies, picking the dirt out of their hooves) are what I miss the most.

We were each assigned a horse to ride every day. My designated horse was Gotcha, an Appaloosa/Quarter and the black sheep of the barn. Aside from the time he chucked me off during a trotting session, we got on swimmingly and I still keep a framed picture of us on my tallest bookcase (we look so good together, I can't decide whether it borders on magic or tragic). Kristen usually rode a glorified pony named Lovebug. "Come on you little runt, yeah, yeah," I would hear her heckle as she trotted past me and the resident Bad Boy. At the end of the two weeks, I won the award for Most Improved Rider. Kristen got Best Bather and was livid. I didn't win a single ribbon in the end-of-summer horse show that Kristen didn't enter. I've thought about getting back into the riding realm, researching stables an hour's commute away in Brooklyn and the Bronx, but my parents aren't footing the bill anymore, and it ain't cheap. A website for a within-city-limits horse rescue operation had a Donate button but listed no contact information. I gave up many moons ago.

Across the gravel from the main barn, where the show horses like Gotcha and Lovebug lived, there was a separate barn housing the frail, injured, or previously abused horses. It was like a homeless shelter without the cots, chairs, colorful personalities, and chaos. Kristen and I usually only walked through it when we needed to sober up from something we had been uncontrollably cackling about. Back then, I hadn't thought it possible to come face to face with horses looking any sadder.

***

Years later, two nights before a New York City Marathon, I walked past an exhausted horse trudging through one of the more picturesque sections of Central Park, head down, hauling a group of oblivious tourists. Every Friday night before Marathon Sunday, there's a kickoff, psych-up event by the finish line in the park, culminating in a fireworks show. The horse freaked out when the fireworks began, neighing, standing on its hind legs, trying to break away from the carriage, eventually racing off in the other direction, carriage still in tow. Horses have sensitive hearing and hate loud noises (a former horse camp leader once said a horse can recognize the footfalls of those he or she has had regular contact with from many yards away—whenever I later crunched through the gravel to visit Gotcha in his stall after school, his reaction made it clear there was some truth to this), and witnessing the intensity of this one's distress made my skin crawl and my insomnia worse. Much like most of the out-of-towners they haul, horses don't belong on the streets of twenty-first-century big cities for long. While on the streets of New York, some have been hit by cars, some have collapsed, and more than one has died. Say what you will about the NYPD, but you'll notice a difference, in body and spirit, if you compare the patrol horses they ride through the middle of Manhattan to the string of Central Park South carriage horses in need of therapy with an anti-depressant or a stiff drink on the side. Don't know why a city cop needs a horse these days, but I do know that those police horses swagger. They walk tall and with certainty, their eyes never looking distant or dead.

My hands aren't completely clean. Pre-horse camp, my family and I once took a carriage horse ride in Québec City because we didn't know any better. That was still the twentieth century, when media coverage was less far-reaching or at least less frequent. I thought nothing of the ride at the time, other than that it was a welcome break from all the walking we'd done in the summertime heat. I try to remember my family's own ignorance and innocence, when I look up into the faces of the people hoisted up in those carriages like emperors.

***

Awhile back, I decided to check out the Blessing of the Animals service at a cathedral about a seven-minute walk from where I lived. I'd thought about going to this annual event for years, but worried how weird it might look to show up without an animal of my own to bless, like hanging around a playground or a Chuck E. Cheese game room without a kid. Nothing of the sort mattered to me anymore. One crackerjack characteristic of the aging process is caring less about how things look as long as your intentions are pure. And this was a church for Christ's sake. They couldn't turn me away.

This became the day I learned that churches can totally put you out if there's a special event requiring a ticket, which I might have had if I had woken up earlier. As I stood around the corner from the cathedral's front steps, watching the animals march in, none looked in need of further blessings. Even the three-legged dog seemed in better emotional shape than I was. These were privileged pets, the Hiltons and Kardashians of the animal kingdom. One princess pup had a bow in her tail and wore a pink Converse sneaker on each paw. The sheep and miniature horses radiated heartiness and contentment, the tortoise and the owls were pompous. This was an actual dog-and-pony show. I eye-rolled and side-eyed behind the barricade, coffee in hand, mind racing, firing off snide comments to the closest security guard, adding this photo-op extravaganza to my list of grievances about both organized religion and Manhattanites. My religious grandmother used to have her priest come over to bless our house once a year or so. Those brief benedictions were beautiful, and precisely what abused, neglected, injured, or simply-just-in-a-funk animals deserve—clergy members spending a day carrying their crosses and swinging their incense around the city, visiting as many local shelters, clinics, and stable yards as time permits.

My childhood dream was to become a veterinarian. While perkier peers elaborately planned perfect weddings, my girlhood fantasy involved heading to Cornell Vet School (*I should be there*, I thought, when I read it was the best in the business), graduating at the top of my class, of course. I would gain expertise in equine therapy and master the art of delivering a cow's baby. Whenever *The Today Show* had a segment on the benefits of pet health insurance or ways to prepare your pig for a hurricane, there I'd be, their go-to talking head. I would wear scrubs every workday, including during the televised interviews. I look at lifelong animal lovers who followed through with their childhood vision of becoming a vet the way others look at Beyoncé. I still sometimes wish I had more of a way with numbers than with words. I wish I were someone whose hands wouldn't shake and eyes wouldn't flood with tears if I had to insert a needle into an animal's warm and still body. Skulking around those church steps, I wished I could figure out how to get my soul to reincarnate as a rich person's dog in my next lifetime. It could use the break and the cuter, cleaner shoes.

***

On a Super Bowl Sunday, the best night of the year to count on getting the grocery stores and public laundromats pretty much all to yourself, the following statement (from NYCLASS, one of the animal protection groups dedicated to keeping hooves off city streets) popped up in my Twitter feed, ruining an otherwise lovely day:

> *Today an umbrella* [that somebody suddenly opened] *spooked a horse...The horse then took off down Central Park South with frantic and scared customers aboard and hit three cars before stopping...Injured pedestrians* [have been] *taken to the hospital.*

> *This is the second horrible accident on Central Park South in the last few weeks.*

The horse, Arthur, had been working on a 30-day trial basis. Immediately after the accident, the carriage horse industry decided to let him go in a way that struck me as more of a termination for cause than a layoff. An industry representative announced they would return Arthur to his previous owners' farmland...located near Cleveland, not too far from my old riding center. According to the activists who held an emergency rally later in the week, this meant he could get slaughtered. A New Jersey animal sanctuary offered to adopt Arthur, providing him with a loving home where he could plan on dying of old age as much as many of the rest of us can. It looks like the Massachusetts sanctuary (endorsed by the carriage horse industry) he was moved to is no longer in business.

In a city packed to the gills with the idealistic and the enterprising, it's safe to assume the average New Yorker you'll pass has an elaborate castle in the sky playing out somewhere inside the head. Mine is to set the Central Park carriage horses free, one by one. After tossing out the driver and detaching the buggy, I would climb up onto the liberated horse's back, gently remove any silly decorative feather from his or her forehead, hold on tight, and gallop it off to peace and safety, as I'd obviously have trusty accomplices with horse vans waiting near the West Side Highway to shuttle the exploited animal somewhere we've pre-approved as a proper home (much less humid versions of those retirement communities in Florida, where a lot of older New Yorkers relocate once they hit a certain age). It could happen. The times we live in have taught me that anything can happen, and not only in New York. If I, for whatever reason, don't get around to fulfilling this initiative in the near future, everyone else has my blessing to beat me to it.

D-Day

I'm not only a woman without an elevator speech, I'm someone who can't bring herself to want one. I'll wing it in that elevator, at that Starbucks counter, during that commercial flight. It will all sound less counterfeit and rehearsed, winning over the influential person I have a limited amount of time to wow with my noticeable lack of guile. I don't need a class or a workshop or a YouTube video to learn improv. How hard can it be?

When it comes to most chance encounters, I'm about two steps above speechless. People who used to ask what my blog was about got some manner of: "What do you mean? It's about my life, or some of the minutiae that makes up my life. I natter on about things I think or that have happened to me. I socially observe. Can you handle sarcasm?" I actually don't know what that blog has been about and this has never bothered me. Please don't let it bother you. Label it yourself, make it your own, see what you can come up with.

So far, my best chance encounter-esque speech is the presentation I have prepared for: "Why didn't you take the bar exam? Why aren't you practicing law?" It's a question, about what may have simultaneously been the strongest and weakest decision I've ever made, I get asked and must answer so frequently that one might wonder how long it took to commit that detailed of a monologue, an impassioned defense, to memory.

A couple of hours at the most.

"Sounds like that's not the first time you've told that story," somebody I considered potentially influential once responded with a smirk, in a tone I'm all too familiar with. Snarkiness has no ground rules. Anyone can give it or get it anywhere, anytime, its best selling point and biggest drawback.

***

Señor D and his f-bombing have played no small role in revitalizing the land of literary fiction. I would do almost everything short of putting my life on the line to get his narrative voice added to the curricula of all high school English classes, to help shake up the traditional lineup of Shakespeare, Dickens, Fitzgerald, Hawthorne, and the other legends who could stand to step aside every now and then. One night, I stood in a long line outside of a bookstore to hear Señor D read from his latest masterpiece, which had been shortlisted for a major literary award. A book signing followed. On a rush-hour F train, I held onto a sliver of the only available pole for dear life, not knowing what to expect, expecting nothing, weak from my latest pangs of hunger and bout of ennui. Although hunger might feel a little worse, either state is heinous on its own. When the two frailties actively integrate, at that juncture when fused frailties morph into a formidable force, too much of what's coming next gets delivered into the wide-open, wily hands of fate.

The address got underway at 7 p.m. I glanced at my watch at 7:15, after I'd been waiting outside for at least half an hour. People were allowed into the store, one by one. If one person came out, one got let in. When two people came out, two went in, and so on, similar to what it was like getting into many New York stores during the height of the city's coronavirus outbreak, but without the face-mask couture. By the time I advanced fairly close to the front of the line, I couldn't tell how far back it went, but it might have gone all the way down this busy block and around whatever street intersects it. It was a line confirming that the person people flocked to has achieved something deeply distinctive and as permanent as is possible.

An alarmingly thin young man, at least five years my junior, guarded the door with an ill-at-ease imperiousness. He, the bookstore bouncer (I wish I could take credit for that one, but the irrepressibly chatty hipsters behind me came up with it first), wasn't used to being in charge and wore it on his sleeve. At some point right before 7 p.m., Señor D had strolled up to the front entrance, parallel to the line, watching the line, alone, a regular person walking down a bustling city street in his lightweight outerwear on a chilly-but-not-cold night, and couldn't have looked more quietly pleased. He joshed around with the bouncer for a minute before slinking inside, and I seemed to be the only one who noticed or recognized him. Nobody shouted or whispered, "There he is, there he goes!" Those glancing over at him glanced away without interest. That's the beauty of being a high-profile writer instead of a high-profile athlete or entertainment personality. You can reach the peak of your craft and still roll into a venue, hosting a standing-room-only event all for you, as unmolested as he just had.

This particular bookstore sat in the middle of a well-read, culturally and economically elite Brooklyn neighborhood. Most of the passersby asking what the hullabaloo was about knew what the name Señor D signified. The two who approached *me* hadn't a clue, so I had some explaining to do.

"Who is all this for"? one asked.

"Señor D is reading from and signing his new book."

"D? What are his books like?"

"He was born in Santo Domingo but grew up in the US. He writes about the working-class Dominican-American experience, or the non-white American experience, I guess. And about feeling like an outsider, an other."

"And you're a Dominican?" she tossed out knowingly, already convinced she had it all figured out. It was more of a slightly inflected statement than a question.

"No," I said.

"Girl, you look it. You look exactly like my friend's husband."

"I get that a lot." A lot of biracial Blacks get that a lot. We get a lot of things.

"I *know* you do."

She looked really Dominican too. That's why I threw the "Santo Domingo" and "Dominican-American experience" bits into the pitch.

"You should read him," I said. "Just as long as you know, in advance, he's edgy."

"Edgy?" she asked, her eyes erupting into a fireworks show. There was no doubt about it—the two of us had mad friendship potential, and I haven't thought that about many people since my mid-twenties. She referred to me as "lucky" (another concept I hadn't associated with my name in years) for standing so close to the front of a line this drawn out. If she had stuck around a little longer, I would have let her sneak into queue with me, and we would have told all who had a problem with it that we were the best of cousins who hadn't seen each other since Labor Day weekend. As the bond progressed, our friends would become friends, our children would become friends, maybe the grandkids too. When we'd hit the streets with her friend's Dominican husband, he and I would incessantly get asked, "Oh my *Gawd*, are you two twins?!"

"Yes," we'd say. "We are."

"She may have been born 14 minutes ahead of me," he'd keep it going, "but that little silver watch she wears must be 14 minutes behind, seeing how she's 15 minutes late for *everything we do*."

Our public would roar. So would we. As we grew older, that stunt never would.

***

It was an honor to finally be let into the store, which meant standing at the back of an indoor, instead of outdoor, horde. While wandering around the Vatican City's St. Peter's Square, I once wondered how the energy of that crowded space might change the moment the Pope starts speaking from his balcony that overlooks it. Something about this faithful, riveted, reverential, tightly packed multitude no longer kept my imagination in suspense. I couldn't see anything, even on flip-flopped tiptoes, other than the backs and heads in front of me. I heard the slow and steady sound of a male voice and assumed it was Señor D's but couldn't hear what it said. It sounded hoarse, as if he were shouting to the masses straight from the throat. Once the horde inched up a little closer toward the front of the room, I heard his voice echo in a way that revealed there must have been a mic. It was D. That's how far back I'd been and how much of a difference a few inches can add to an experience in a room with restricted audio capacity.

As a fledgling writer, I had done two public readings of my own before, both at the once-great Linger Café & Lounge (not too far from this bookstore), which has since gone out of business. I remember getting super into it, loving the way my voice synergized with the mic, lifting as slowly and certainly as D's did in this larger, better-known venue (although this place later went out of business too).

Oh no. I'd inched up into the middle of a Q&A session. "Why did you have characters in the book saying nigger instead of nigga?!" an old boy, who could pass for Dominican as much as I can, a few rows ahead of me yelled out. The faithful can be so judgmental. This was even worse than, "How do you come up with your ideas?" or "Is there a special snack you eat while you write?" "Which lucky charm do you keep on your desk?" "Do you write in bed?" Homeboy slaughtered the reverential vibe, and for what? Take me back to St. Peter's Square. "Nigger is so much more aggressive than nigga," he continued. "And then you use Dominican slang."

An author bothering to respond to any anti-artist question with something less crass than, "Oh, because I can. My book, my choice. If you don't like it, stop reading it, don't recommend it to others, text a friend about how much you think it sucks—leave me and leave it, find someone who will type out 'nigga' instead of 'nigger' and meet your other specific preferences," confirms how much benevolent patience still runs rampant in this digital, post-MTV era.

That night, Señor D read a short passage from his new opus. It was so damn hot at the back of the horde and there I was, hungry and dehydrated, worrying about passing out in public, something I've done before and haven't wanted to do again. Any minute, my stomach would start protesting, audible to all.

Five minutes later, there was a break in the horde. The masses made way for two bookstore employees who walked, then carried, a bespectacled, profusely sweating, bulging-eyed, disoriented intellectual out of the store (book tour events held during traditional mealtime hours should be lightly catered by the corporate publishing houses; just a little something—mixed nuts, baby carrots, maybe some Teddy Grahams), while I tried to maintain my composure and wondered how someone as talented as D internally reacts when he reads the writing he's released to the public, months and years later. I wondered if he ever cringes or doesn't think it's all that great, even if smart people whose opinions he respects are impressed; if he believes he could have done it better without nailing down how. When I was younger, an older, wiser stranger on the Washington Metro—who hadn't seen me in the act of reading or writing—once approached me to ask if I was a writer almost a year before I officially recognized myself as one. Has D had a similar encounter? Does he belong to that camp who believes you're not allowed to call yourself a writer until the writing is what pays the bills, the only occupation you list on your tax returns, and you've been made privy to a secret handshake? These are a few questions I could ask if I ever got him alone in an elevator and we had more than a minute to kill.

Whenever I tell anyone I'm an editor and a writer, they only want to talk about the writer part. I care more about what I've written than what I've edited.

I once participated in a creative nonfiction workshop I had, going into it, been exceedingly excited about. I had recently read one of my workshop leader's books, and was so bright-eyed and bushy-tailed to build a bond with her. This workshop instructor, from the very beginning, made it clear she wasn't remotely excited about me or my writing. To the point where I guess you could say she was a little harsh during a review of my essays. "You're not that smart!" she cried out at one point.

Seeing as how I'm more of a snowflake than others may realize, I initially walked away from that experience questioning whether I should ever write for an audience again. After not working on any writing outside of my personal journal or my blog for about two months, I eased back into revising my essays from the workshop, incorporating the substantive portions of that candid tutorial, such as introspectively revealing more of myself instead of just reporting on things that happened, and not being too coy with points I'm trying to make. I deeply revised or completely scrapped all the other essays I'd written, fueled by that advice. Everything I've written since then has benefited from that advice. That workshop instructor has played a supporting role in my becoming a better storyteller, as have most of the people and places I've had exposure to. Years later, I found it more than fitting that the finale song from *Les Misérables* began blaring out of my earbuds the moment I noticed the email accepting my first longform personal essay for publication (although this place has, you guessed it, now gone out of business too).

***

The formal speaking part of the night segued into Señor D's book signing, which led to another line to stand in, this one serenaded by Radiohead songs whining out of a weak sound system. The conditions weren't much different from bargain shopping at the 125th and Lenox Avenue Marshalls, in the heart of Harlem, with non-stop Goo Goo Dolls, Third Eye Blind, and Gin Blossoms ditties (*"tomorrow we can drive around this town/let the cops chase us around"*) seeping from hidden speakers while Blacks and Latinos push shopping carts and strollers, looking pissed off as hell.

On some level, I hadn't completely processed that the end goal would happen, that I'd actually make it up there, to D, face to face. Or that this was a goal of mine at all. At another packed book signing, for a bigger and much different celebrity, almost 10 years earlier, the crowd was at least as large as this one. When I advanced to the head of that line, a very old man was the only person who stood between me and the author. The author and one of her aides suddenly broke the momentum to privately confer about something. Maybe it was about how tired she was, or how she needed to be somewhere else soon, or how she'd spur-of-the-moment decided she was sick of being A-list famous with everybody always wanting something from her, or possibly all of the above. She and her crew took a look at those of us standing in the rest of the line—the elderly man; me; a mom and her two tween girls who had driven up to this Washington, DC, venue from one of the Carolinas; maybe a smattering of others behind the three of them. After many other hopeful ones had been sent away at least an hour earlier, all of us who were allowed to remain in the line had been told we were guaranteed to meet Her. And we believed it. "He'll be the last," the author abruptly announced about the guy in front of me as she waved him forward. She signed his book, stood up, and marched off. The Carolina kids took it better than I did, and it's this sort of bullshit I've come to expect at every crowded book signing since then.

A standoffish young woman who stood next to me during D's reading was under the impression she could cut ahead of me in his signing line, where she swiftly reappeared next to me, like we were together. Single file meant nothing to her. She'd scowled her way through most of the reading, with an energy so disagreeable that when she disappeared immediately afterwards, I forgot about how famished I was and focused on the soft and sweet wind that swept over me once she was no longer a physical part of my space. The wind turned sharp and squally the instant she silently returned to my side. A gal pal of hers later joined us. It sounded like they might have been in an MFA program, although they could just as easily have been a couple of wet-behind-the-ears local undergraduates. "We should get to read whatever books we want, instead of having books assigned to us," the new person declared. The friend agreed.

This was enough inspiration for me to consider rehearsing some elevator speeches, to consider supporting those things. All I had was time and a desperate need for useful distractions. Behind us, a sea of hipsters sounded off, and in such rapid fire. They must have stopped in for some fair-trade coffee, pre-lineup. No topics were off-limits:

So what do you think of D-Day?

Converse sneakers were a bad call tonight.

Did you feel the same way about King Arthur?

Which book are you getting signed, man? None, dude. I'm just gonna talk to him.

I didn't have earbuds or earplugs—just another 45 minutes in this line. Rehearsing elevator speeches it was:

Elevation #1: Now Señor, it wouldn't kill me to have a writing mentor—it would make me stronger. One whose name I could, but wouldn't, drop. What would it take for you to take a chance on me for free? I'll workshop you if you workshop me.

Elevation #2: The first book review I published was about your first novel. When my dad read it, he told me how proud he was of me, and he doesn't use that gushing of a tone in reference to something I've done very often. Not long after the review dropped, I mailed you a photocopy, along with a nice, light message on a Post-It note. You never responded. I'd

*hoped that review, and your blessing, could be my big break
and it wasn't. Where, pray tell, do you suggest we go from here?*

Elevation 3: What do you *think of D-Day?*

After a lot of thought, I leaned heavily toward #2, or a
variation of it, because of the emotional risks that were
taken. I've been told I don't take enough of those, even
though it feels like emotional risk-taking is all I ever do.

So what happened next? I finally reached D, and still
don't know how things went so south, so fast. Face to face,
he's the spitting image of the happy-hour-shift host from
the restaurant that used to sit in the lobby of my former
office building. I was thrown.

"Congratulations," I kept saying.

"Thank you," he kept responding.

He signed his name to each book that came to him,
without asking for the signee's name. It wasn't even his
name he signed—he inked out his big, loopy initials, as an
autograph is nothing more than a source of amusement for
some people.

"Thanks for coming," I think he said.

While he drew, I talked. "Back when I was writing
book reviews, this [his first novel] was the first review I
published," I said.

He became visibly intrigued. *I'm so good at this,* I
thought. *I have him right where I want him.*

"Really, where?"

When I told him the name of the publication, his intrigue visibly evaporated and, I mean, *please*. I find it very hard to believe that this guy didn't have to start somewhere too.

"You're one of the only sisters who reads my books," he claimed, half-laughing, as I started giggling hysterically. His view of the horde from the podium must have been as limited as much of the horde's view of him. But here was someone who could tell I'm not Dominican. His laser eyes intently watched me, en route to accurately sizing me up. This threw me too. Some of the creative types are like walking polygraph machines, only the kind that nobody could outfox.

We shook hands more than once. When I reached out my hand for what was most likely the third time, he refused to accept it, stepping back and looking at me with a Now That's Enough firmness. Throughout that whole exchange, I chewed gum, may or may not have stuttered, and hope only one bra strap was showing, but I was feeling pretty good as I walked off in a daze. Alright, so strong improv isn't a cakewalk and I could use a seminar. Or a 'round-the-clock chaperone, one who will remind me that those you connect with on paper, on a stage, or on the screen won't always want to link arms with you when your bodies and souls find themselves three inches apart. And vice versa.

On the C train coming home, I stood at the rear of the very last car, looking out the back window, traveling through the cellar of my city. A window glass reflection, of my subway car and the passengers in it, interfered with my view of the semi-lit-up tracks. Everyone seated in the most fluorescently reflected row appeared to have suffered a recent, unforeseen defeat. Another one. Their stoicism had a shelf life. The sight of their sadness made me antsy, it made me want to get home and write. Not necessarily to write about how sad they looked, just to write, period, in detail, about everything I could remember having seen, done, faced, picked up on. As I homed in on my own image in the glass, expecting my mug to mirror theirs, the relaxed smile on and in my face disarmed me.

LIVING OF NATURAL CAUSES

Some women get their nails professionally done once a week. Others do it once in a while. I've done it once (like, in total), the day before a lavish wedding on Long Island. When the manicures menace has featured into other wedding- or bachelorette-weekend itineraries, I've gotten out of them (either staying behind in my apartment/hotel room or wandering the streets), keeping an eye on my watch or phone to avoid running late for when the time came to rejoin the group for the eating and drinking portions of the celebration. But I was *in*, quite in the thick of, this particular wedding. All who have served know that bridesmaid duties, especially when you're a bridesmaid living in the same metro area as where the bride lives and/or the wedding is taking place, come with heightened expectations to remain extra-accommodating and keep the antisocial antics to a minimum.

When it came to this manicure, the mother of the bride insisted on both the pampering and paying for everything but, in the interest of keeping it real, no one twisted my arm. My curiosity got the better of me. I kind of liked nail polish and the idea of some firsthand "mani" experience because this was when I was still down for trying anything and everything I hadn't tried before, as long as it didn't cost me much money. The freer the better. If someone had offered me a complimentary weeklong stay at a crocodile petting zoo that summer, I'd probably have shrugged and said sure, as long as there was air-conditioning.

"Isn't this fun, sweetheart?" the mom asked, sitting regally at the nail station to my right, perfect posture, offering her hands up with dainty, insuppressible glee. My own mom had died two years earlier. In the aftermath of her death, this person (who was nothing like her) was a much-needed older woman who cared enough to step up as a mother figure for me, as best she could.

"I guess," I said, holding back a grimace. The manicurist's attention to my cuticles seemed unnecessarily rough, and I could tell she could tell I'd pull my hands back if she didn't hold on tight. The procedure, the production, took forever. A pedicure came next. This was not the kind of salon I've seen on cable reality shows, where they hand out wine or champagne to make it easier to smile or forget. About *one hour* later, the finished products, my hands and feet, looked no different from when I do my own nails, in my pajamas, while watching cable reality shows revolving around ladies who treat beauty parlors as their second homes. I may not, on my own, paint all 20 of my nails very often, but when I do, they look just fine.

Many women wear makeup every day, many wear it on special occasions, and at least one woman has only worn it during a brief phase in middle school. It was never around the house to play with or learn from since neither of the other ladies in residence, my gray-haired mother and white-haired grandmother, wore it. In fact, my mom was adamantly against my (and everybody else) wearing it, thus all the more incentive to take it up. She never forbid makeup. She never really forbid me from doing all that much, preferring to just passionately rant about most of what she didn't like every chance she got, which I'll take over banning something any day. Although she slipped up every now and then, she was a tireless advocate for concepts like substance over image, and a foot soldier for the *au naturel* lifestyle, which included vehement opposition to artificial sweeteners like NutraSweet. Since the taste of NutraSweet/aspartame-ridden diet pop had grown on me, I figured I'd acquire a taste for the makeup too. Friends and acquaintances had started wearing it, giving the whole shebang—the extra morning chore, pulling out a compact or tube of lipstick before class, owning and replenishing the contents of pretty pastel makeup bags—a rite-of-passage sheen.

A number of mornings in a row, I woke up half an hour earlier than usual, while it was still dark outside, to put on my face before school. Drugstore foundation and powder. Blush, even though my cheeks have no problem staying pink without intervention. There may have been mascara. (Lee Press-on Nails made an appearance during another brief, unrelated phase, and as cool as they looked, I lacked the poise or patience to keep all 10 glued on for long.) I threw a CoverGirl or Maybelline compact with packed powder into my purse to continually check in on the new exhibit, my face a full canvas, debating whether it needed tweaking or updating.

Christ, was it exhausting. The earlier mornings, smearing it all on, drawing everything in, staying within the lines, having to be more careful about touching my face and rubbing my eyes. Feeling like a doll or a sculpture until I was finally able to wash the goop off. Jail time for the face.

Jumping onto this bandwagon did not change my life for the better. In that era, I was far from physically or socially blessed. Overweight, unfashionably dressed, teeth covered with braces, not much of a follower but by no means a leader. The makeup brought no seismic shift, not even one in my head. There was no uptick in my confidence or sense of self. The boys I hoped would like me for something other than my mind or my sometimes-sweet disposition didn't seem to notice or care about the new façade. The resident It Girls paid no more attention to me than usual. An enormous relief now, if not then.

At a Halloween carnival that week, someone's mom, who wore heaps of makeup every day, not daring to leave home without it, was the only one to comment on and compliment my work. I wish I could say her words meant something to me, but I didn't, and still don't, want to look more like her. I hated the way it felt, smelled, lightened the color of my skin. This was my costume to that carnival, which marked the end of my experimentation with face painting. Experimentation, even for me, has its boundaries. Despite some lingering curiosity, I have yet to experiment with hardcore drugs (I'm afraid I'll like them too much). Cosmetics and cocaine (or whatever they're doing these days) can seem like such must-haves for the supposedly coolest crowds, maybe a ticket to more lively and colorful experiences at first, or in the moment, but too much of a financial and emotional burden once you get hooked.

***

That sweltering summer morning of the Long Island wedding, the bride's mom also treated the bridesmaids to a team of amiable makeup artists who came to the bridal suite in the hours leading up to the outdoor ceremony, for which we all wore long black dresses. I can be amiable too, and provided each artist with no shortage of good-natured extra company and conversation while they worked on every woman in the room except for me.

I'm still impressed with myself for not having passed out once we stepped outside. It was that hot and sunny, and my sleeveless dress was that long, thick, and black. With the sweating, wooziness, and dehydration that out of control, makeup would have taken my frame of mind over the edge, and I'm glad to have put my foot down about this one, to have been one of the only bare-faced women (although it really might have just been me) at the indoor, air-conditioned reception. I think we might all agree how startling it can be to see someone we've only ever seen fully made up without makeup. I find it equally startling to see someone (such as this particular bride) who usually doesn't wear it with it on. Taking in the never-before-seen blood-red lips and teal eyeshadow, I turn into my mother: *She looked better without it.*

It's about more than just looks. I also deal with extremely sensitive skin on my face and lips, and have had allergic reactions to many over-the-counter products, including sunscreen and Chapstick. This doesn't keep me from wearing and needing lip glosses and balms. My most beloved has been a $3 tub of jasmine-scented petroleum jelly I found at an Indian grocery store in a suburban strip mall. I've more commonly walked around with a tiny plastic container of Vaseline ("that lip gloss looks so good, where'd you get it?" more than one has asked in passing) in my bag instead of $8 lip treatments from Sephora or that brand of balm that's a dead ringer for an Easter egg. Every Christmas morning in middle school and high school, one of my most-anticipated gifts (better than the clothes and electronics, almost as good as the jewelry and books) was a plastic cylinder (festively topped off with the head of a reindeer) containing three different flavors (Dr. Pepper, cotton candy, maybe strawberry or watermelon) of Bonne Bell Lip Smackers, the kind of scented lip nourishment I continue to use, although Cleveland-based Bonne Bell no longer runs Lip Smackers so these newer models don't feel as sacred to me. For years, when I said I'm breaking out the good lip gloss, I meant my fragrantly fruity Bonne Bell rollerball number, designed for the angsty yet playful teenager at heart.

Although my daily moisturizing and regular exfoliating (sometimes with a homemade scrub—one tablespoon of sugar, one tablespoon of baking soda, two tablespoons of water) have a cosmetic effect, I consider these skincare routines more health-based than aesthetic. I put loads of superfoods, super-spices, and water into my body instead of Botox. In between all the sighs and tears, I have laughed a lot, and the creases around my mouth and eyes confirm it. Why go out of my way to erase or cover up signs of the *good* memories? As someone who now prides herself on knowing how to read people, I prefer to look into their eyes. Not at the lines around their eyes (those lines are called fine for a reason), or at other parts of their skin, or at what they're wearing, or at anything else that can't help me sense how gentle they might be at their core.

A street salesman in Italy once assured me he could tell that a handbag was real leather by attempting to burn it, whipping out a lighter to demonstrate that the bag in his hand couldn't be set aflame, proving its indestructibility (this bag I bought from him turned out to be a fake, though not a total disappointment, like so many people whose names we have programmed into our phones). Another, much more legitimate, salesman in the same town said he could tell that a piece of leather was real by noting the imperfections, that imperfections signaled quality.

***

What about hair? Some women get theirs professionally blown out, dyed, straightened, or at least professionally cut, on a regular basis. I've received flyers in the mail advertising $150 foil highlights, Brazilian blowouts, and balayages ("the most popular hair coloring request in salons today," a Google search explained).

I'm my own hairdresser; my bathroom is my sole salon. The only product going into the Afro I've worn since birth is shampoo, no conditioner. Preferably a brand that runs under two dollars a bottle (a full year's supply for such a little head of hair like mine)—Suave, V05, White Rain. I've made audible scenes ("Da *fuck* they want from me?") in drugstore aisles upon noticing a local pattern of jacking up these brands' standard asking prices from $0.89 to $1.09 or beyond. Growing up, my dad cut my hair for me in our living room, usually on Sunday nights or nights before I went back to college, while I sat in my grandmother's squeaky wheelchair so he could more easily swivel me around, an old and fraying towel draped around my neck and shoulders, *60 Minutes* or shows such as a phenomenal (and unpardonably short-lived) 1980s NBC weekly musical comedy-drama called *Rags to Riches* often on the TV in the background. "Stop fidgeting," he would say whenever I lost my tolerance for sitting still or jerked my head around to try seeing more of what flashed on the screen. "Do you want to lose an ear?"

In my early twenties, I started cutting and styling my hair myself with the aid of a pair of junk-drawer scissors and a bathroom mirror. Afros are so easy to cut and maintain, I feel sorry for those who don't have one. I love not having to fret over the idea of getting it wet each time it starts drizzling, love that no amount of wind or humidity can make it look any less, and can't blame anyone who asks to touch it. *Well, at least I don't have any of* that *to worry about*, I think whenever I glance inside the hair salons I walk by. Trimming my hair takes me no more than 10 minutes. No more than one minute if I'm only doing a couple of spot touch-ups.

The life I lead is like everyone else's—littered with problems, issues, inconveniences, post-traumatic stresses, ceaseless errands, sporadic windows of luck. Something has sure had to give. My disinterest toward most cosmetic customs began because I couldn't be bothered, couldn't bear one more task on my list. Laziness as much as liberalism. I also sweat and cry too much to wear even waterproof makeup without incident. Since I've always practiced social distancing from hair, nails, and eyebrow appointments, New York's coronavirus lockdown wasn't nearly as frustrating for me as it evidently was for many others.

I'm amazed at the amount of upkeep it can take to be considered a presentable woman, including the publicized tips for creating a more minimalist "no-makeup routine," involving a fake rosy glow by way of an easily blending cream blush. I don't even upkeep that much, and still get drained from the little I do. Women have been socialized to frown upon frown lines, to devalue and denormalize their original states. "As you grow older, as a woman [any woman who wants to experience anything unboring, not just women in showbiz] you'll need makeup and other potentially expensive, chemical-filled crap to get ahead," was something nobody said but the consensus made clear. Over time, my outrage mounted about how only men can go to work or out to dinner or to a party without feeling any pressure to revamp their faces first, that only they have the right to bear bare faces.

Some women might love wearing makeup, reporting to an eyebrow-sculpting appointment, balayaging their hair. Some men might too. Makeup artists should compare themselves to Michelangelo; I've seen them create some serious masterpieces. It's art, just not the art for me, like a lot of that Renaissance stuff. I love jewelry, headbands, scarves, and henna because I love to decorate and most of these forms of physical self-expression don't compromise the well-being of my skin, hair, body, or time. I wear and accessorize with as much pink, purple, and pastels—Power Colors—as possible. When I rush out of my apartment and realize, two blocks away, I forgot to put on any jewelry, I think about turning around to go get some but rarely have. The first time this happened, I felt naked but got used to it later in the day, after refocusing my energy elsewhere. Whenever I start getting upset at the thought of how much money I've blown by living in New York all these years (instead of somewhere much more affordable), and the other financial hits I've taken, I rechannel that guilt into tallying up all I've saved (possibly tens of thousands of dollars by now) by generally, politely, ignoring the "beauty" industry's services, products, and "goodies." I can't be the only one who believes that a "goody" has got to be edible.

I've been told that my untouched eyebrows are bushy (FYI, the bushier brows are now, at the time of this writing, all the rage), but go well with my overall vibe—the one softly screaming out that I've never really been much more than a girl who would rather be listened to than looked at, a woman longing to live of natural causes.

ACKNOWLEDGMENTS

Sometimes I can't believe I managed to finally sit down and finish getting this essay collection in strong enough shape to confidently submit it to publishers. Although I didn't submit the manuscript to *publishers*—I submitted it to one publisher. I could tell that Unsolicited Press was the best home for this content within moments of reading its website copy. Thanks to the whole team, with particular applause for my kind and perceptive editor, Jay Kristensen Jr.

I have an extra-special appreciation for: my family members (those who still remain in this world and those who now belong to the spirit world); Kristen Korpa; Rhonda Binda; and every single person who read/reacted to early drafts of these essays, over the years. Sure hope my next book is midwifed into existence with as much tender loving care as this one was.

ABOUT THE AUTHOR

Originally from Cleveland, Ohio, Kadzi Mutizwa now lives in New York City. *Living of Natural Causes* is her first book.

ABOUT THE PRESS

Unsolicited Press is rebellious, much like the city it calls home: Portland, Oregon. Founded in 2012, the press supports emerging and award-winning writers by publishing a variety of literary and experimental books of poetry, creative nonfiction, fiction, and everything in between.

Learn more at unsolicitedpress.com. Find us on twitter and instagram: @unsolicitedp